The
Greaseless
Guide
to Car Care

Mary Jackson

John Muir Publications
Santa Fe, New Mexico

Special thanks to Dave Hoefel, Red's Automotive Services, Albuquerque, New Mexico, and John Forsdale

John Muir Publications, P.O. Box 613, Santa Fe, NM 87504

Second edition. First printing September 1995

Library of Congress Cataloging-in-Publication Data
Jackson, Mary, 1946–
    The greaseless guide to car care / Mary Jackson. — 2nd ed.
        p.   cm.
    Rev. ed of: The greaseless guide to car care confidence. 1st ed. 1989.
    Includes index.
    ISBN 1-56261-212-3 (pbk)
    1. Automobiles—Maintenance and repair—Amateurs' manuals.
I. Jackson, Mary, 1946– Greaseless guide to car care confidence.
II. Title.
TL152.J275   1995
629.28'72—dc20   95-18369
                                                            CIP

Copy Editors: Julie Lefevre, Dianna Delling
Production: Kathryn Lloyd-Strongin, Sarah Horowitz, Janine Lehmann
Design: Kathryn Lloyd-Strongin, Sarah Horowitz
Illustrations: Maria Voris and William Rotsaert
Typesetting: Marcie Pottern
Printer: Publishers Press

Distributed to the book trade by
Publishers Group West
Emeryville, California

Contents

Preface

"Garage-ese" is a language developed and spoken by motor-heads to other motor-heads. Unfortunately, it is also spoken to non-motor-heads. This book has been written and revised to close the communication gap between the two. It is exclusively for those who may never tune or troubleshoot but who, nevertheless, would like to be able to speak confidently, to understand, and to be clearly understood when it comes to buying a car or having a car repaired, and further, who would like to avoid unnecessary repairs and overcharges while getting the longest serviceable life out of their automobile.

As the only girl growing up in a family of five boys, I did not learn garage-ese at home. Information about cars was placed on a "need to know" basis, and in our family, girls did not need to know.

That worked fine until I began driving my own car. I quickly discovered that I had a definite need to know. I had a need to know about new sounds coming from my car. Did they mean a $2 or a $200 repair? Or should I begin looking for a new car? I had a need to know about routine maintenance. Was I doing the right thing by checking the engine oil every leap year? I had a need to know about repairs and pricing. Was I being treated fairly, or did service providers identify my obvious ignorance as fair game? Having almost no knowledge of my car and no language with which to learn about it, I struggled hopelessly with repair explanations and in the end, reluctantly and blindly delegated full responsibility to mechanics. My vulnerability, frustration, and sense of powerlessness ended when I moved to a small Vermont town and, in an effort to avoid starvation, took a job in a local body shop.

There, among the tack rags and paint fumes, while doing general repair work, I had my first opportunity to look inside cars. Engines, transmissions, and brakes began to make sense as I peeled back the outside and observed their basic parts and relationships, all the while, like a three-year-old, asking hundreds of "why" questions.

This book is intended to pass on my learning experience, sans paint fumes, with the hope that knowing the basics about cars will help you to open the door to car care confidence as it has done for me. And by the way, in case you were wondering, I am not now, nor will I ever be, a true motor-head. There are days when my correcto-tape dispenser challenges me. I have never set a VCR, and my microwave cooking is limited to boiling water and defrosting my morning English muffin.

This book is not an exhaustive work, but rather a framework for building car care confidence and providing protection from car repair rip-off.

I would like to thank Dan Donza for opening up the world of cars to me and for helping me in too many ways to mention to make this book possible; and Lenny Bisceglia for his knowledge, time, patience, and unique explanations of how cars tick; and to the many others who contributed in some way to my assembling this information. I also want to thank the many fine companies and technicians throughout this country who have provided me with technical information. Thanks also go to the participants who have attended my workshops. Their humor, intelligent questions, and insightful comments have been an invaluable help.

I am very fortunate to have as my publisher John Muir Publications. And Maria Voris' and William Rotsaert's illustrations have made the words come alive as I had always hoped they would, with clarity and humor.

Speaking of words, I owe much to Ray Fry, a true car guy, who patiently helped me find the right ones. His love and knowledge of automobiles is an inspiration, and I am truly grateful for the enormous amount of time and effort he devoted to this edition. I want to thank my friends for continuing to support me at all levels and in the most wonderful and generous ways, but especially for their intelligent and insightful feedback to early versions of the guide. I want to thank my brothers, Danny, Lenny, Mike, Kevin, and Mark, for being the very funny men they are, and for teaching me the invaluable place of humor in my life and work. There is also my other family, the Marshalls, whose love and encouragement continue to make a huge difference. A special thank-you goes to my husband and friend, Jim Marshall, who contributed in every imaginable way to helping me write this book, but especially for convincing me that I could.

And finally there are my parents, the late Leonard and Pat Horan, who taught me that any limits I would encounter in my life would be self-imposed, and that there is no knowledge that is either inappropriate or unattainable.

1
Introduction

Cars play an integral part in our lives. Most of us depend on them every day, and we invest large parts of our paychecks in their upkeep. Fortunately, cars only seem mysterious, and the more you know about them, the better off you'll be. This chapter sets the stage for using this easy-to-understand guide to car care. It shows how making yourself "auto-literate" can help protect you from car repair rip-off and keep you safer on the road. You'll discover how to spend less on service while providing your car with all the TLC it needs to go the distance, free from the repair bills for the rich and famous. ❖

Sometimes all you can make out of a repair bill is the massive total. With knowledge, you can protect yourself from unnecessary charges.

Your car has been making weird noises, but you'd rather watch a continuous loop showing of *The Man with the Synthetic Brain* than visit your local repair facility. Finally, after turning up the radio a few times, you bring it to a repair shop to be fixed. You carefully explain the new sounds, and the service writer nods sagely and tells you, "No problem. Pick it up at 4:00." Later in the day, you arrive to pick up your mechanical steed and you're handed a bill that's completely illegible, except for the $475 total. You don't know what to do.

You're running a few minutes late for an important appointment. You jump in your car, turn the key, and nothing happens. You don't know what to do.

You're driving down a lonely highway and you get a flat tire. There's not another car in sight. You don't know what to do.

Powerlessness. For many people, it's a familiar feeling when dealing with the everyday problems of owning and driving a car. Consider the importance of the automobile in our lives. Most of us depend on our cars every day; they are essential to holding down jobs and running our busy lives. A car is likely to be the second largest item in our budget—the largest, if we don't have a home mortgage.

Yet what really goes on under the hood of your car may be as mysterious as the transporter on the *Starship*

Cars are complex, yes, but also systematic and, with a little study, understandable.

Enterprise. Why is it so mysterious? Is it understandable only to those with special knowledge and powers of perception? Can only a select few learn its hidden secrets? Of course not.

Car Mystique

Most of us didn't get together with our pals to give the old Chevy a tune-up, unless we grew up in a family where some member was a backyard mechanic. If we weren't shown the differences between a V-8 and a slant 6, we just didn't get to learn how cars tick. For women, this missing part of our education was informally institutionalized into learned dependency: someone would always come along and take care of these mechanical objects for us. But we were never sure who that someone would be.

For many years, our ignorance didn't really seem to matter. During the 1950s and 1960s, a few giant-sized domestic manufacturers sold us cars, while local service stations, staffed by mechanics we knew and who knew us, fixed most things that went wrong. There was some degree of accountability, or so we hoped.

By the 1970s, the number of independent garages had begun to shrink. They were replaced by sterile self-serve stations that sold everything from microwave burritos to baseball cards—but not service. Government agencies issued regulations to control our cars' harmful pollutants. Auto manufacturers responded with smaller cars that ran on more fuel-efficient engines and produced fewer emissions. With more and more cars jamming the highways, and more laws limiting toxic emissions, the auto industry turned to advanced electronics to enhance their cars' performance and safety features.

From the halls of high technology came the automotive computer. An electronic "brain" in the form of a little black box replaced traditional mechanical parts. Computers' lightning-fast accuracy burned fuel more efficiently, thus eliminating even more pollutants while improving

The automotive computer—an electronic "brain" in a little black box—has replaced many traditional mechanical parts.

the power and performance that had initially been sacrificed for economic and environmental concerns. With complex computers came complex diagnosis and repair. Our automotive lives would never be the same.

Small shops very often could not afford the costly diagnostic equipment and Manhattan-telephone-book-sized manuals that were required to decipher the workings of the newer cars. Nor could they keep pace with the constant influx of technical information. The independent shops that had been the backbone of the repair industry were replaced by automotive specialists (including car dealerships) that only worked on certain types of cars and by large franchises that only fixed certain types of components like brakes and mufflers.

Knowledge of garage-ese has become increasingly important in communicating about our cars to service providers.

Our ignorance of the automotive animal was beginning to take on a new and different significance. The repair person who had known our car intimately and intuited that when we said "shimmy" we really meant "vibrate," who knew when we scrinched up our faces and made a sound like a crazed bumblebee that the speedometer cable needed lubrication, who knew every time our car was on the lift to inspect it thoroughly for hidden problems we weren't expected to know about—that person was gone. Repair shops now employed legions of mechanics. Often we never even saw the person who worked on our car, or had the opportunity to tell him or her what was wrong.

Speaking Garage-ese

We now had to negotiate with intermediaries. Knowledge of "garage-ese" (car lingo), which had never seemed very important before, became increasingly necessary, but no less frustrating, to understand and to speak. We were like tourists visiting a foreign country with no knowledge of the language, no understanding of the currency exchange rate, no map. . . . On arriving in the capital city, we ask a taxi driver to take us to a nearby ruin. The trip seems to take forever. Did we cross another border on the way? We finally arrive, hand the cabby a fistful of the local currency, close our eyes, and hope that we aren't going to be taken for another kind of ride.

The Good, the Bad, and the Indifferent

As our cars have become more complex, we have become increasingly likely to delegate responsibility for them to strangers, hoping that we won't be taken advantage of, at least not too much. Sometimes putting all the responsibility for our welfare in the hands of strangers works. Sometimes it doesn't. It backfires when repairs are diagnosed incorrectly, are not done right the first time, are done when unnecessary, or are done appropriately but at an outrageous cost. When it comes to our cars, the real issues are often not so much mechanical as financial.

It's not that all the members of the automotive repair industry are involved in some plot to take advantage of us. It's just that in every field, there are the good, the bad, and the indifferent. If we don't have a basic understanding of how our cars work and a command of the basic principles of autologic, we are unable to tell the difference. When we can't tell the difference, we are at the highest risk of being overcharged, sold service work we don't need, and being faced with not getting a problem fixed the first, second, or sometimes even the third time.

A basic understanding of how cars work can help you avoid unnecessary or overpriced repairs.

What a different trip it might have been had we arrived in that "foreign city" with a pocket dictionary of important phrases, a calculator to compute the exchange rate, and a good map of the city. We might not have known that the cabby had taken us a few blocks out of the way to make a few more dollars, but we would have known if he had decided to circle the entire town before dropping us at our destination. And we would have known if the fare was reasonable given what we knew about the exchange rate. This book is the equivalent of a pocket dictionary, a calculator, and a reliable city map.

Cars are too complex for a book this size to make us fluent in the native language. The car has an average of 12,000 parts, 1,500 of which move, including at least one on-board computer and dozens of emission control components, most of which can create symptoms similar to those produced by many other systems. Fortunately, we're in luck—cars are logical and systematic. Just as with all systems, if you begin with the basics, they can be broken down into small pieces and eventually understood.

A car works something like a bicycle. In both, up-and-down power is converted into rotational power.

Cars and Bicycles

A car works something like a bicycle. When the bicyclist pedals, she generates up-and-down power through her legs. That power makes both the bicycle chain and the wheels turn. Up-and-down power is converted into rotational power, and down the road the bicycle goes.

Inside each car's engine there are three or more round metal plugs called **pistons**, which are attached to a round metal bar called the **crankshaft**. Like the bicyclist's legs, these pistons move up and down. Their up-and-down power makes the crankshaft turn, which, through the **transmission**, turns the car's wheels. Once again, up-and-down power is converted into rotational power, and down the road your car goes.

Just as the bicyclist needs a balanced diet to perform

Your car's engine needs a balanced diet of air and fuel to generate power, just as the bicyclist requires food.

❖

well, so does your car's engine. Instead of carbohydrates and protein, a car needs air (the kind we breathe) and fuel (gasoline). These elements are combined in the right proportions and compressed in the hollow tubes (**cylinders**) that house the pistons. When a hot spark is added at just the right time, it's like dropping a match into a container of gasoline. *Boom!* Because the air/fuel mixture is compressed, it doesn't simply burn, it explodes and expands, releasing its energy. The expanding gases push the pistons down with force. Because the pistons are attached to the crankshaft, their movement causes the crankshaft to spin and, eventually, the wheels to turn.

Just as the chemical energy of the bicyclist's body is converted into the mechanical energy of the bicycle's wheels, so is the chemical energy of the exploding gases converted into the mechanical energy of the moving pistons, crankshaft, and eventually the car's wheels. If the bicyclist's diet is unbalanced—for example, if she forgets her green vegetables or eats too much sugar and not enough carbohydrates—eventually she begins to feel unwell, and her bicycling performance suffers. She just doesn't have the energy to generate the power that she did when her diet was correctly balanced. Hills that were once a piece of cake now look like Pike's Peak.

Likewise, cars also suffer if their diet is unbalanced.

Air + fuel + fire = Power

As the air/fuel mixture explodes and expands, it pushes the pistons down, causing the crankshaft to spin and the wheels to turn.

❖

Too much air, too much fuel, or a spark that is not hot enough or delivered at the wrong time will result in poor performance. Hard starting, lack of acceleration, stalling, surging, hesitating, and low gas mileage are all symptoms that may be related to an unbalanced diet.

The Proper Care and Feeding of Your Car

Cars suffer if their diet is unbalanced.

Preventive maintenance is linked to a proper diet. Your car can't go out and buy what it needs to take care of itself. It needs you to do that by periodically scheduling routine maintenance. Just as you regularly visit your dentist to have your teeth examined, cleaned, and repaired when necessary, checkups and adjustments are necessary for your car. It takes a professional who knows how to perform a precise series of tests and adjustments to maintain the correct proportions of the car's diet so that it runs smoothly and economically. Furthermore, parts must be repaired or replaced as they wear out or break.

In addition, routine maintenance fights two enemies that arouse dread in the heart of every car: dirt (the garden variety) and friction. **Friction** is the abrasive action that results when two pieces of metal rub against each other. Friction results in the wearing away of the metal. If correct preventive maintenance is not performed on time, dirt and friction can cause a lifetime of expensive repairs and can send your car to an early grave.

Just as people are equipped with filters (liver, kidneys, and so on) to keep our systems free of contami-

Routine maintenance helps combat two enemies of car health: dirt and friction.

❖

nants, so are cars. Air, oil, and fuel are just a few of the many filters that keep the dirt that is naturally present in the atmosphere from invading and damaging the finely machined parts of your car's engine and its other systems. Like any home heating filter, a car filter must be replaced at regular intervals in order for it to continue to perform effectively.

Dirt and foreign particles can clog the tiny openings or passageways that carry essential fluids to their destinations. If dirt reaches the moving metal parts of the engine, it acts as an irritant. Like a piece of sand in an oyster shell, the dirt scratches the smooth surfaces of the engine's internal parts, causing them to wear prematurely. Unlike the oyster, you won't get a pearl, but you can count on a gem of a repair bill.

Cars and people need fluids to survive. Without oil (engine and transmission), coolant, brake fluid, power

Don't become a car abuser. Have your auto serviced regularly.

❖

steering fluid, and other liquids, your car wouldn't last any longer than you would without an adequate supply of blood and water. Automotive fluids, which are circulated through hoses driven by pumps, perform many jobs, including holding contaminants in suspension, lubricating and reducing friction, and controlling the offspring of friction—heat.

Because cars are idiosyncratic, there is no one right maintenance schedule for all cars. The appropriate schedule for your car is found in your owner's manual. There you will find two service categories, "severe" and "normal." Read the description of each carefully to decide under which conditions you usually drive your car. Most of us fall under the "severe" category since we do a lot of stop-and-go driving. By keeping your car on its service schedule, you spend a limited amount of money every year in order to avoid spending unlimited amounts of money later on the repair or replacement of prematurely worn parts. A well-maintained engine uses less fuel, thus making some contribution toward paying for itself.

About your owner's manual—most of you probably have yours sitting by the bedside table, within easy reach, so that you can go over and over those particularly fun-filled pages. You know, the dog-eared ones? No? You haven't read it? You took it out of the glove box

Granted, it's no page-turner, but your owner's manual contains essential information about the proper care and feeding of your car.

❖

once, during a blinding snowstorm, to find out how the defroster worked?

Nobody can blame you. Next to insurance policies, owners' manuals are the dullest of dull reading material. That fact notwithstanding, they contain extremely important information about your car, information that is seldom available anywhere else outside of textbook-sized repair manuals. Furthermore, it is probably the only free information you're likely to get which explains your car to you. Critical pieces of information such as whether your car can be pushed, pulled, or towed without doing damage to it can be found in your manual. Cars that get pushed, pulled, or towed in ways they're not supposed to be can require additional expensive and unnecessary repairs.

Your owner's manual also has information such as the specific requirements for replacement fluids. Put in the wrong weight oil, for example, 10W-30 instead of the manual's recommended 10W-40, and the warranty may be voided if an oil-related engine problem develops. The result may be both embarrassment and unnecessary expense. Furthermore, a fluid that is good for one car is not necessarily good for another. What your neighbor's car wants may be entirely different from what yours requires; that is, unless you both have the same make, model, and year. In that case, you can opt for the true pinnacle of owner's manual intimacies—you can read it together.

Critical pieces of information about your car's care can be found in your owner's manual.

If you don't have an owner's manual, contact the parts department of a car dealership that sells your type of vehicle and ask them to order one for you. Expect to pay a small amount.

So put down that best-seller and add a brand new dimension to your reading. And when you're done, put your manual in the glove compartment where it's handy. It's a valuable source of information and a vital key to the reduction of your car care vulnerability.

Car Care Confidence

It's time to re-evaluate the system. You may not want to change your own oil, or replace an air filter, or attend automotive school, and you don't have to. There are honest and competent professionals ready and willing to work on your car. This book will help you to learn to recognize them and to deal with them when you find them.

Finding a good mechanic is essential, but it is not enough to ensure good car care. Even the best mechanics are not magicians or psychics or even private detectives. You can't expect to drive in with your ailing auto and say "It's broken," then have your mechanic know exactly what's wrong and fix it immediately for a reasonable price. Before your mechanic can diagnose or fix the problem, he or she needs to know what symptoms have brought you and your car to the garage.

Understanding how your car works will help you when talking with a mechanic. Reading your owner's manual and learning the basics about how cars work are good strategies to protect yourself from unneeded, phony, or overpriced repairs. Once you understand how the basic systems work, you can use everyday language to communicate with your mechanic as long as you are clear, accurate, and thorough in describing your car's symptoms. When you know what a fuel injector is and does, you will be better able to discuss its problem and how to solve it. You will also be better able to understand the explanations of what was found and what was done. Knowledge is your protection. It is how you can empower yourself.

To begin, take the idea that cars are mysterious and throw it out the nearest window. And with it, toss the argument that computers have made cars too complex to be explained or understood by anyone other than technicians. A computer in your car operates as a computer does in the rest of your life: data in, data out. Computers have taken over specific jobs that were traditionally done by mechanical components. If you understand the traditional job of ignition, for example, then you can make the leap to a computerized ignition. It's simply one more layer to digest mentally and understand.

Shifting from the passenger's to the driver's seat when it comes to car care depends on accessing meaningful information. It can be confusing to reconcile the clearly defined manufacturer's recommended maintenance with the seemingly endless variety of tune-ups and other work that is offered by various service facilities. If the person with whom you communicate about service for your car—the service writer or technician—thoroughly understands how your car works (and why sometimes it doesn't) and has the skill and the intention to translate the technical terms into English, you are far more likely to have a satisfactory relationship with your car. Whomever you choose to service your car, base your choice not only on their technical competence but also on their ability to communicate technical information to you effectively.

Use this book to unlock your car's logical secrets; they are yours for the asking. Knowing about cars will enable you to understand what your service provider is really saying, and it will make it possible for you to make your car last longer without the repair bills for the rich and famous along the way.

This book covers in a logical order all the systems of the car. Each section describes how a system works, what you can do to make it last longer, what you need to know if something does go wrong, and a list of common troublemakers.

If women have been mechanically uninformed in the past, it was only because we did not see the need to be otherwise. Learned dependency, the teaching that someone else (presumably a male) would come along and take care of our cars for us, was informally taught.

In my own experience, as a kid growing up, whenever there was a problem with a car, my five brothers, Danny, Lenny, Mike, Kevin, and Mark, would run out to the car, lift the hood, and begin discussing at length the virtues of carburetors, distributors, and spark plugs. The message I heard while I stood watching from a distance was that I did not need to know about cars. Excellent, I thought, one less thing for me to worry about. It was excellent—until I was out on my own and got my first car. Then I found that the system was fatally flawed. I hated a trip to my mechanic because I never knew if I was being sold repairs that I didn't need at inflated prices. So when I would hear a new ka-thunk coming from under the hood, I did what many others do when they hear those new ka-thunks coming from under the

Before I was auto-literate, when I heard a strange ka-thunk coming from under the hood, I did what many others do when they hear a strange ka-thunk: I turned up the radio.

hood. I turned up the radio. The ka-thunks eventually turned into ka-thuds, and inevitably it cost me money.

Things changed for the better right after college, when I took a job in a local body and fender shop. There among the paint fumes and twisted metal, I learned that my five brothers knew less about cars than any other

The more you know, the less money you'll spend and the longer your car will last.

❖

five human beings on the face of the earth. More important, I learned that cars were both logical and understandable. And the more I learned, the less money I spent and the longer my cars lasted. I still can't record with my VCR, but I love my cars, and they last a long time. And when I buy maintenance and repairs, I am confident that I am buying only what my car needs at a fair and honest price. I did not have to don battle gear and become She-Ra, the twin sister of He-Man, Master of the Universe, to do it. This book is designed to help you do the same.

Times have changed. Both women and men have equal access to the power, excitement, and freedom of cars. Both women and men need to be autoliterate. It is simply too costly not to be. Whether it is choosing the right gasoline and oil to minimize expense and extend the life of your car, understanding the warranty before and after you buy, or simply being able to communicate about problems in a way that makes you comfortable and confident, you need to know about cars.

Knowing about cars is a right, but rights have to be exercised. It's not always going to be comfortable to assert those rights, especially in the beginning. But just in the act of buying this book and deciding to take charge of your car, a personal and empowering change will take place. A flat tire on a lonely road—once a horrible night-mare—will instead become only an inconvenience. Now you know what to do.

2
Air and Fuel:
The Diet, Parts 1 and 2

This chapter describes how the car's "diet" of air and fuel is delivered to the engine and includes tips on how you can avoid expensive repairs to fuel injectors. It's all you ever wanted to know but were afraid to ask about gasoline, including how to choose the right fuel for your vehicle. ❖

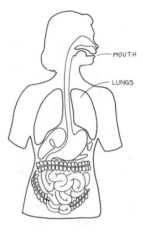

A car's air-intake system is analagous to the lungs. The fuel-intake system can be likened to the mouth.

The air and fuel systems

❖

"**Carburetor**" was just one of the "secret" words that was knowingly thrown around by my brothers as they poked their heads under the hoods of the cars parked in front of our home. As a kid, I placed such words in the "unknown" category. For me, that meant not only unknown but "unknowable." It was as if there were a secret club, and I was not a member. When I finally learned what a carburetor is and what it does, I discovered it was no big secret, and there was no exclusive club.

How Carburetors and Fuel Injectors Work

The definition of carburetion is "to combine chemically," and for many years, the carburetor was the system of choice for combining the first two parts of the engine's diet: air and fuel. In recent years, though, carburetors have been replaced by **fuel injectors**, the carburetor's faster and more efficient computerized cousin. Most vehicles built today are equipped with **fuel injection**. This does the same job as a carburetor but provides more power while permitting the engine to run on a mixture that is both cleaner (friendlier to the environment) and leaner (uses less fuel in proportion to air).

The carburetor is actually a food blender for your car's engine. It draws measured amounts of air from outside the car and combines it, in a very special way, with measured amounts of gasoline drawn from a tank in the rear of the car (as far away from the engine's spark as possible). This mixture is then distributed to the cylinders, the stomach of the engine.

In the carburetor, the liquid gasoline is transformed into a fine spray, similar to the mist produced by an atomizer. By making the gasoline molecules smaller, the carburetor turns the gasoline into a vapor.

Vaporized gas, which burns more easily than gasoline in its liquid form, is exactly what the doctor ordered. When vaporized gasoline burns, its heated gases explode and expand, pushing the pistons down. This causes the crankshaft to spin and the wheels to turn, and is the "combustion" in the internal combustion engine.

In the carburetor, liquid gasoline is transformed into a fine mist. In this new form, gasoline burns more easily.

Electronic Fuel Injection

There are two types of electronic fuel injection (EFI): throttle body and multi-port. **Throttle body fuel injection** looks like a souped-up carburetor that is missing its insides. It sprays a common measure of the fuel down to the engine, where it is distributed along a spray bar to each cylinder in equal amounts.

In **multi-port fuel injection**, a separate injector acts like a hypodermic needle, squirting a small amount of fuel into each cylinder. To give you some idea of how miserly this fuel metering system is, consider the microscopic hole through which the fuel is delivered. It's about the width of a human hair, and so tiny it has to be made with a laser beam! Even if you have thick hair, that's a very small opening. Nevertheless, the result is more power and less pollution.

A whiz-bang on-board computer, an electronic brain, is responsible for ensuring the success of the fuel injection system. This microprocessor, often called an electronic control unit (ECU), receives information from

The fuel injector opening is about the width of a human hair.

THROTTLE BODY
TYPE INJECTION

MULTI – PORT
TYPE INJECTION

Throttle body and multi-port fuel injection are the two types of fuel injection found in today's cars.

The fuel injector acts like a hypodermic needle, squirting a tiny amount of fuel into each cylinder.

❖

sensors (electronic eyes and ears) located throughout the car. The sensors feed back information about many things, including the speed of the engine, the temperature of the air, and the density of the air and gasoline. With this input, the computer then determines the best ratio of air and fuel. To learn more about how these computers work, turn to chapter 7.

Air Filter

Cars require an enormous amount of air to breathe. About 9,000 gallons of air are needed for every one gallon of gasoline used. By anyone's reckoning, that's a lot. It is important for the smooth running and long life of

your car that the air it breathes is clean, that is, free of
dirt and dust. It is the job of the appropriately named
"air cleaner" to do just that.

A breather hose, commonly called a snorkel, actually
carries the air from outside the car into the air cleaner. En
route, it is heated by hot air that has been redirected
from the engine by the **pre-heated air-intake** system. The
air passes through the air cleaner, a container that houses
the **air filter**—the workhorse of this cleanup detail. The
air filter, which is made of pleated folds of paper, catches
dirt and dust before it can get down into the finely
machined engine parts.

Just like any home furnace filter, the air filter must be
changed when it's full. Most cars need a new filter about
once a year, every 15,000 miles (24,000 kilometers), or
whenever your owner's manual recommends. If you
happen to live in the Sahara, or merely on an extremely
dusty road, you will probably want to change your air
filter more often.

For years the air filter could be easily found under
the hood. Checking and changing the filter was the classic do-it-yourself chore. Anyone who wanted to save a
trip to the repair shop could check the air filter merely by
removing a couple of clamps and performing a simple
test. You would just remove the filter and hold it up to a

AIR FILTER

AIR CLEANER

Most cars need a new air filter about once a year.

light; if light could be seen coming through one side, the filter was still in good shape.

As hood designs have been lowered, though, air filters are now found in a wide range of sizes, shapes, and colors and are located in several different areas within the engine compartment. Some manufacturers now advise that the air filter should only be removed by a trained professional. They warn that the flow of air to the engine may be interrupted if the filter is positioned incorrectly when it is replaced. If the airflow is interrupted, the car may run roughly or not at all. A few dollars savings may turn into ten times that much spent on a visit to the repair shop to correct the problem.

A dirty air filter can increase fuel consumption by 10 percent.

If do-it-yourself isn't dead, it sure is breathing hard!

How Fuel Is Fed to the Engine

To get the gasoline from the rear of the car to the engine, a **fuel pump** (usually more than one), located either in the gas tank or between the tank and the engine, pushes the gasoline along the **fuel lines**, which lie along the bottom of the car. Until the 1970s, fuel pumps were mechanically driven by an attachment to the turning engine. The majority of fuel pumps manufactured today are electric. Within the tank there is also a device called a **sending unit** that monitors the amount of gasoline and sends that information in the form of electronic impulses to the gas gauge located on the dashboard.

On its way to the engine, the gasoline passes through one or more **fuel filters**, miniature versions of the air filter, which catch dirt and foreign particles before they reach the working parts of the carburetor or fuel injectors.

A fuel filter may be small, but it's mighty. This tiny filter is responsible for cleaning the many gallons of gasoline that pass through it and should be changed regularly to ensure peak performance. The fuel filter in most cars should be changed about once a year, every 10,000 miles, or whenever your owner's manual says.

FUEL PRESSURE REGULATOR

FUEL INJECTION

COMPUTER

ELECTRIC FUEL PUMP

FUEL FILTER

Fuel is fed to the engine by a fuel pump, which pushes gasoline along the fuel lines to the fuel injector.

❖

Important Facts About Fuel

As teenagers, my five brothers and I used the family car, so it was common in our house to hear Dad yelling as he slammed the front door, "Who used the damn car last? And why didn't you put gas in it?" Mercifully, often by the time he recited the litany of all our names, he had forgotten the infraction. There's no telling how many times he was stranded because of our selective reading of the gas gauge.

After I graduated from school, I began driving my first car. It was a little black Volkswagen that I dearly loved and still remember fondly. And it taught me a lot about gasoline.

Despite the fact that my Bug got about 172 miles to the gallon, I habitually refused to put in more than 47 cents worth of gas at any one time. This had much to do with the fact that I never seemed to have more than 47 cents to spend at one time. Furthermore, using the skills I had learned as a teenager, I meticulously estimated exactly how much gas was in the tank at any given time. Using these calculations, I frequently arrived at a gas station with little more than fumes in the tank. The car would struggle, sputter, cough, and die in front of the pump, and I would emerge triumphant, congratulating myself for doing another swell job of squeezing every last drop out of the tank. I then pumped in another 47 cents worth and off I'd go for two more weeks. It was not until several years later that I discovered what my calculations had really wrought.

Now, take a look at the illustration of the fuel tank. See those little dots at the bottom of the gas tank? Those harmless-looking specks are actually pieces of dirt and contaminants that gradually accumulate at the bottom of any gas tank. The particles rest there, harm-

As a teenager, I perfected the art of running on empty . . . and had no idea what it was doing to my beloved Bug.

❖

less, until the fuel level in the tank gets so low that the fuel pump sucks them out along with the last few drops of gasoline.

To continue the story, every time I arrived at the station with the gauge on "empty," the dirt and other contaminants at the bottom of the tank had been forced along the fuel lines to the fuel filter, which quickly clogged and needed replacement. As a result, I bought a lot of unnecessary fuel filters and paid for several tows and a carburetor cleanout!

Even after I discovered the expensive consequences of my 47-cent habit, I couldn't seem to quit. Desperate, I began to pretend that if the tank showed a quarter of a tank, it was actually empty. I am happy to say I am

Pieces of dirt and contaminants accumulate at the bottom of the gas tank and are pumped out to the fuel injectors along with the last few drops of gasoline. The moral? Gas is not "good 'til the last drop."

Money-Saving Tip

If you live in a cold climate, avoid **gas line freeze-up** by keeping your gas tank as full as possible, especially at night. Condensation causes water droplets to form inside the gas tank. On days when the temperature drops below freezing, water droplets can turn into ice crystals that move along the gas line with the gas and clog the flow of gasoline. The less space in the tank, the less area in which condensation can form. Be particularly careful during the spring and fall months when condensation is increased by greater daytime-to-nighttime temperature fluctuations.

On very cold days, water droplets in the gas tank can turn into ice crystals that move along the gas line with the gas and clog the flow of gasoline.

finally cured. Now I habitually practice the second
nicest thing anyone can do for a car: keep the tank as
full as possible. (I'll tell you the first nicest thing you can
do for your car in chapter 8.) Remember, gas is not
"good 'til the last drop."

Choosing the Right Gasoline

The **octane rating** of a gasoline (the number displayed on
the side of the gas pump) refers to its resistance to
knocking or **pinging**. Ideally, gasoline should burn
smoothly and evenly throughout the entire combustion
chamber. If the gasoline has too low an octane number, it
may burn roughly or explode at the wrong time, subject-
ing the engine to vibration. The engine will still run, but
it will wear more quickly.

The sound you may hear coming from the engine is a
metallic rattling that is called pinging or knocking. It

**The octane rating of a gasoline refers to its resis-
tance to knocking or pinging. The higher the
octane, the smoother the gasoline will burn.**

❖

sounds like metal marbles or ball bearings rattling
around together. The higher the octane, the slower and
smoother the gasoline will burn and the less likely it is to
burn irregularly and cause knocking or pinging.

Should you buy super unleaded gasoline? Not necessarily. To know for sure if you should be paying the extra cents per gallon for premium unleaded, read your

Gasoline that has too low an octane rating may burn roughly or explode at the wrong time.

❖

owner's manual. If you find it recommends premium unleaded, or a gas with an equivalent octane rating, use it. The manufacturer's advice is based on its extensive experience with your engine. In other words, like it or not, your car's engine may simply require the more expensive premium unleaded gas for engine performance that is knock- or ping-free. But if your owner's manual recommends the use of regular or mid-grade, don't bother with the higher priced gas.

If you're already using premium unleaded and you still hear pinging or knocking, it's a good idea to have the car checked out by a professional. Some pinging is normal in newer cars and is considered an acceptable trade-off for the fuel efficiency. Excessive pinging or knocking, however, can cause engine damage. If there's any question in your mind about your car's ping, rattle, or knock, ask your service provider to decide by road testing your car.

Your car may knock or ping if you choose a gasoline with an octane rating that is too low.

Octane rating is like shoe size. If you have a size eight foot, wearing a size ten shoe won't help you run any faster.

Frequently asked questions

Q How do I calculate my car's fuel economy?

A 1. The next time you buy gasoline, record the odometer reading. 2. Drive until there is about a quarter of a tank of gasoline remaining. 3. Record the odometer reading again. 4. Fill the tank and record the amount of gasoline you buy. 5. Subtract the first odometer reading from the second odometer reading and divide the sum by the number of gallons (liters) of gasoline you bought. The answer is your miles per gallon (kilometers per liter).

Clean Air Fuels

It would take approximately 25 of today's cleaner burning cars to pollute the planet at the same rate that just one pre-emission-control vehicle of the '50s or '60s might have done. Nevertheless, pollution remains a growing concern for society, government, and the automotive

Just one '57 Chevy polluted as much as 25 of today's cars.

industry. The gasoline industry is currently attempting to modify ordinary gasoline to respond to the demands of the government's turn-of-the-century deadlines for cleaner air.

One solution is to modify gasoline to burn cleaner. Some gasoline is currently being reformulated with additional oxygen. These extra oxygen molecules cause the gasoline to burn more completely, and more cleanly. Among the most popular of these oxygenated fuels are **ethanol gasoline** and **MTBE**. Ethanol gasoline is organically based; it's made from grain. MTBE is a synthetic version; it's made in a chemist's laboratory. *Note:* As long as the additives in specially formulated fuels are in proportions approved by your manufacturer (check your owner's manual), they are considered to be harmless to your car and friendly to the environment.

Ethanol is an organically based oxygenated fuel additive that helps gasoline to burn more cleanly.

In the meantime, experimentation continues with alternative fuel sources. Public acceptance, high cost, engineering problems, and, in some cases, an inadequate distribution system are just some of the hurdles encountered when introducing alternative fuels to the marketplace. Technological and distribution problems may restrict alternative fuel use to fleet vehicles, such as buses, taxis, and delivery trucks. Right now, it's anybody's guess. Following are some of the alternatives being considered.

Methanol is made from natural gas, coal, or biomass (wood chips or garbage). Starting difficulties in cold weather with straight methanol require the addition of some gasoline. A common proportion is 85 percent methanol and 15 percent gasoline.

Methanol is a potentially plentiful fuel.

Compressed natural gas, like oil, is created by the decay of plants and animals over millions of years. Liquid petroleum gas (LPG), also known as propane, is extracted from natural gas or is a byproduct of refining petroleum. LPG vehicles are far more common in Canada, where the distribution system is more mature. In the United States, LPG is currently not readily and consistently available through the existing network of service stations.

Electric vehicles draw their energy from battery packs. Currently, however, electric vehicles are limited by the technology of today's lead acid batteries (the same kind that are found under the hoods of our cars). The challenge has been to create a battery pack that can provide adequate power for an extended driving range (without excess weight), adequate acceleration features, and sufficient service life (presently, the expensive batteries must be replaced after only a few years of use). Longer life batteries made with exotic materials could change all that.

The most promising and practical alternative fuel system appears to be a hybrid vehicle. Most hybrids combine an electric system with one other system for longer range driving. A variation of a hybrid is a flex-fuel vehicle, which is designed to allow the driver to switch to whatever fuel is convenient—ordinary gasoline or any combination of gasoline and methanol (or other alternative fuels) in the same tank.

Electric vehicles draw their energy from battery packs.

Frequently asked questions

Q What is "vapor lock"?

A The additives in today's gasoline have raised their **volatility**, which is the ability to change from a liquid to a vapor. During hot weather, gasoline may actually boil, causing it to stop flowing. The result is **vapor lock**: the engine is deprived of fuel, and lets you know with symptoms such as rough running, loss of power, and, in some instances, stalling.

Modern electric fuel pumps located far from the heat of the engine provide more constant pressure to the system and have alleviated the problem in most cars. But if yours isn't one of those, and vapor lock is a problem, try switching from your regular brand of gasoline to another reputable brand. If that doesn't work, it's possible that the fuel lines can be rerouted so they are farther removed from the hot spots of the engine.

Making your car go the distance
Fuel Delivery System

If you follow a few simple rules, you'll help your fuel delivery systems last. Preventive maintenance with these systems is essential.

✓ Air and fuel filters trap dirt and dust and must be changed when they are full. Most cars need a new air and fuel filter about once a year, every 15,000 miles (24,000 kilometers), or whenever your owner's manual recommends.

✓ The microscopic openings of fuel injectors require squeaky clean gasoline. To avoid fuel-related performance problems, buy a reputable brand of gasoline to be sure that you're getting the best quality detergents.

✓ Try changing gasoline brands to solve minor engine performance problems. The additive packages of each major brand are different, and some cars "like" one better than another. After you fill up, look for any change, for better or worse, in the way the car drives.

✓ Fuel injectors and carburetors need periodic cleaning and/or adjustment. But hire a trained specialist equipped with up-to-date equipment and service manuals to work on your fuel injectors. Check your owner's manual for service schedule specifics.

Troubleshooting the Air and Fuel Systems

Symptoms	Dirty air filter	Cold enrichment system	Dirty/faulty carburetor	Dirty/faulty fuel injectors	Fuel pressure*	Contaminated fuel	Incorrect octane	Air (vacuum) leak	Vapor lock/hot soak	Idle speed control system	Computer-related**	Fuel leak
No start/hard start–cold	●	●	●	●	●	●		●			●	
Hard start–hot	●		●	●	●			●	●			
Stalling/hesitation–warm	●		●	●	●	●		●		●	●	
Stalling/hesitation–cold	●	●	●					●		●	●	
Rough idle	●		●	●	●	●		●		●	●	
High idle		●						●		●	●	
Surging		●	●	●				●			●	
Knocking/pinging (on acceleration)						●	●				●	
Afterfire (dieseling)		●	●				●	●				
Backfire		●						●				
Poor fuel economy	●		●	●							●	
Black smoke/tailpipe	●	●	●	●							●	
Lack of power	●		●	●	●			●			●	
"Check engine" light on				●	●			●		●	●	
Gas fumes		●							●			●

*Fuel pump pressure could be fuel filter, fuel pump, fuel pump pickup, fuel pressure regulator, fuel pump drain valve, restricted fuel line.

**Computer-related symptoms can be caused by the computer itself, its wiring and connection, or one of many sensors including mass air flow sensor, coolant sensor, throttle position sensor, crankshaft sensor, oxygen sensor and many others not listed here. Before beginning computer diagnosis the technician should inspect the engine, mechanical, electrical, and fuel systems.

3
The Spark: Ignition and Charging

The ignition and charging systems provide the spark that gets a car started and keeps it going. This chapter describes how these systems work and makes recommendations that can help ensure that your car starts every time, runs more reliably, and gets better fuel economy. You'll learn about the life and death of batteries, what a tune-up is, and when to get one. ❖

The ignition and charging system

❖

DIGESTIVE JUICES

The ignition system can be compared to the human body's digestive system: both break down the components of a diet, and both release energy that is converted into motion.

"Ignition," once I had learned its meaning, was another automotive term that convinced me that cars were not mysterious. Ignition comes from the word *ignite*, to set on fire, and what better device for setting something on

The igniting spark journeys from the battery to the coil and on to the distributor, where it is "dealt" to the spark plugs. There the spark ignites the air/fuel mixture.

❖

fire than a spark? The job of your car's ignition system, therefore, is to add a spark to the explosive air and fuel mixture that the fuel delivery system has taken such pains to create.

How the Ignition System Works

The journey of the spark begins at the **battery** and ends at the **spark plug**. If anything interrupts it along the route, the car will not start at all, will start with difficulty, or will run roughly.

When you turn the ignition key, it sends a wake-up call to a small (12 volts) electrical **current** that has been resting in the battery. Those 12 volts aren't much in electrical terms (your home generally uses 110 and 220 volts), but before their journey is over, they will have been magnified many thousands of times.

When activated by the ignition key's wake-up call, the small particles within the battery begin to move around in a solution of water and chemicals called **electrolyte.** It is this movement that will be converted into electrical energy, or current.

From the battery, the 12 volts travel to the **coil**, where they get a big boost. The coil turns those puny 12 volts into a fortified spark—40,000 to 50,000 volts of electricity. That's enough voltage to curl your hair without a curling iron.

From the coil, the spark moves to the **distributor**, which acts like a card dealer. The distributor deals an equal portion of the spark to each cylinder. There a spark plug receives the spark. This very hot spark now jumps,

IGNITION KEY

BATTERY

FLYWHEEL

CRANKSHAFT

STARTER MOTOR

The starter gets things going by turning the flywheel, which turns the crankshaft, which moves the pistons up and down.

❖

or **arcs**, across the gap at the tip of the spark plug. The spark flashes, causing the air/fuel mixture to explode. *Kaboom! Kapow! Kapooey!* The spark's entire journey, from battery to spark plug, takes place in a fraction of a second!

Getting a Good Start

At the same time the ignition key is sending a message to the battery, it is also sending another signal to the **starter**. This small but powerful electrical motor starts things off by moving the pistons up and down until the first explosion takes place and the engine turns over.

The starter's distinctive feature is a small, round, metal-toothed wheel, or **gear**. Attached to this gear is an arm called a **solenoid**. When the ignition key is turned to "on," the solenoid pushes the gear forward so that it meshes with a large heavy disc called the **flywheel**. The flywheel is attached to the **crankshaft**, the metal bar that holds onto the pistons. The flywheel also has teeth in the form of its **ring gear**. When the flywheel turns, the crankshaft turns. When the crankshaft turns, the pistons move up and down.

As soon as the flywheel begins to turn, the starter's job is finished. It pulls itself back and away from the rapidly turning flywheel in order to avoid decapitation!

At a time when electricity is pretty much taken for granted, electric starters hardly seem worthy of special notice, but without them, our automotive lives would look very different. Think about this: Before modern

Money-Saving Tip

To keep its electrical system healthy, give your car a break from stop-and-go traffic and drive it for 15 to 20 minutes at highway speeds. Doing this once a week revitalizes the charging system. It's the equivalent of giving your car a good aerobic workout.

starters were invented, cars were started by manually turning a metal bar or crank that fit into a socket in the engine. It was often necessary to repeat this back-breaking task many times—50 to 150 hand cranks were not uncommon—before the engine would start. An incorrect grip or a backfire, causing the crank to jump back on the cranker, could result in a broken thumb, arm, or jaw, with an occasional hernia thrown in for good measure.

The Charging System

A battery doesn't make electricity; it only stores it—much like a checking account stores dollars. Once the battery gets the engine running, the **alternator** takes over.

The alternator generates the electricity that provides power to all the electrical systems in the car while the engine is running. The alternator also sends to or "deposits" power in the battery while the car is running to recharge the battery's depleted electrical supply. In this way, the battery is always ready to start your car.

The **voltage regulator** acts as an auditor, controlling the flow of electrical power to and from these devices

The charging system works like a checking account: the battery stores and "spends" electricity, the alternator makes deposits of electrical current, and the voltage regulator audits the flow.

and ensuring that the battery is neither discharged nor overcharged by the alternator.

As is true of many of the components in your car, the alternator is activated by a belt that runs on a pulley, similar to a clothesline pulley. The belt is attached to the turning crankshaft. Whenever the engine is running, the

Frequently asked questions

Q What should I do if the alternator light comes on?

A The good news is it's probably not fatal—just massively inconvenient. The rule is to keep driving until you reach a service station. Turn off as many electricity-draining accessories as you safely can. The hardest thing the electrical system has to do is start the car, so *don't turn the engine off unless it's absolutely necessary.*

Warning! If the temperature light comes on at the same time the alternator light is on (or simply by itself), stop the car as soon as you can. The same belt that drives the alternator often drives the water pump. If the water pump stops working, it won't be long before the engine overheats and its internal parts melt. The result will be major damage and expensive repairs.

An activated alternator or battery light means more electricity is being used than is being replaced.

belt turns and the alternator makes electricity to recharge the battery and to power the accessories. However, the alternator only fully recharges the battery when the car has been driven for approximately 5 to 20 minutes at highway speeds.

Belts

Cars have from one to five belts under the hood. Many newer cars have a single **serpentine** belt that drives all the accessories. Belts transfer power from the engine to various components, including the alternator, water pump, power steering pump, and the air conditioner. As belts wear, they stretch and get thinner. As the thinner belt sinks deeper into the pulley, you may hear a high-pitched squeaking sound or a squeal (an extended version of a squeak) coming from under the hood. Incorrect tension causes the belt to wear faster, and may cause the component it drives to malfunction.

Belts transfer power from the engine to various components.

Computerized Ignitions

Today almost all cars have **electronic computerized ignitions**. The same engine computer that provides a better air/fuel mixture has also taken over coordinating the functions of the traditional ignition system. Many of the

Almost all cars today have computerized ignitions.

traditional ignition components, including the coil and the distributor, have been replaced by electronic components. Sensors feed back information to the computer so that it can determine when the spark should arrive and how hot it should be when it gets there. (For more about computers, see chapter 7.)

The Tune-up

A tune-up is the routine replacement of spark plugs, filters, and other air-, fuel-, and ignition-related parts, plus a precise series of tests and adjustments to regain maximum engine performance and fuel economy. For today's cars, this includes a computerized engine analysis that uses hundreds of tests to compare the car's performance with the manufacturer's standards.

Today's tune-up includes a computerized engine analysis that uses hundreds of tests to compare the car's performance with the manufacturer's standards.

Depending on whether it's minor or major, a tune-up may also include battery service, timing adjustment, idle speed adjustment, vacuum and compression checks, pollution control systems inspection, and the inspection of belts and hoses. What is included will depend on the make, model, and year of your vehicle, but the result should always be a quick-starting, smooth-running engine that gets the best possible fuel economy.

A tune-up does not include an oil change (or even an oil check!), nor does it include a brake inspection, tire rotation, wiper blade replacement—or tightening the screws on your license plate. While you may find it very desirable to get these maintenance chores done at the same time you get a tune-up, you will probably have to ask for them.

You won't find this information under the heading of "tune-up" in your owner's manual. (What you *will* find is a list of things all good car owners ought to do every so many weeks, months, years, or miles/kilometers— otherwise known as "scheduled service.") If the service in question is supposed to be done every 7,000 to 30,000 miles (12,000 to 50,000 kilometers), and it directly concerns returning your car's engine to maximum operating performance (air, fuel, and spark), it is probably part of a tune-up.

The Life and Death of Batteries

As with most things in life, a battery ages and grows tired with use. The chemicals in the electrolyte are eventually absorbed into the interior walls or **plates** of the battery, where they form a hard, crusty deposit. These deposits first appear as a white powdery substance on the terminals that protrude from the battery's top or side. Eventually these deposits block the passage of the electrical current.

When the plates become completely covered, the battery discharges and can no longer provide the necessary electrical energy to start the car. If the battery is not too far gone, an electrical current is run through it in the opposite direction (a charging direction) by a battery charger, and the deposits disappear from the plates and return to the electrolyte. The battery may get a new life.

Eventually, however, all batteries die when they run out of chemicals, the plate deposits become too extensive, the plates vibrate and break apart, or the outside casing cracks.

The white powdery substance that collects on the battery terminals eventually blocks electrical current.

A battery's efficiency is dramatically affected by the temperature. On a very cold day, a battery may lose up to 80% of its ability to provide a spark, while it may take twice the energy to start the car.

❖

If you live in a cold winter climate, you may want to consider investing in an engine or battery heater, which can decrease the power needed to start a car.

Batteries also hate the cold. When the outside temperature is 80° F (27° C), a battery is 100 percent efficient. On a cold day, that same battery at 0° F (-18° C) is only 40 percent efficient. At -20° F (-29° C) it is only 18 percent efficient. In other words, more than 80 percent of its ability to store the electricity needed to start the car is temporarily absent! Just as important, when the temperature drops below freezing, it may take as much as twice the energy to start the car.

For a healthy battery with lots of chemicals left in it, there's usually no problem. However, for an older battery that has used up a lot of its chemicals, losing 80 percent of its starting ability—when it didn't have too much to begin with—may be the last straw. Have your

Money-Saving Tip

Batteries should be recharged slowly whenever possible. Incorrectly recharging a battery can destroy both the battery and expensive electronic accessories such as digital clocks.

battery inspected during a pre-winter check, so it won't leave you in the lurch when the snow flies. If it needs to be replaced (see below for more about replacement), have it replaced then by someone you know and trust; don't wait until the freezing cold morning it fails to have it replaced by the tow-trucker who will probably only have one battery to sell you—the million-dollar brand.

Making your car go the distance
Ignition and Charging Systems

If all the systems and their component parts are in working order, a car is said to be tuned correctly. The sound you will hear as you turn the ignition key is "vrrooon-vrrooon," the muffled sound of many explosions and the mark of a smooth-running engine. If not, you may hear a lot of "rrreh-rrrehs" before you finally get a "vrrooon-vrrooon." If things are really fouled up, you may hear no sound at all. Following are important facts about the ignition and charging systems that can help make yours more reliable and trouble-free.

✓ Hot starts may require more battery power than cold starts so restarting problems can occur when the engine is hot. Pay extra attention to your battery's maintenance if you live in a warm climate.

✓ Don't make your starter work harder by turning the ignition key for more than 30 seconds; the excess heat will send it to an early grave. Allow cool-down periods between starting attempts.

✓ Before replacing a battery, have a competent technician inspect all ignition and charging components—they may be the real culprits when a car won't start.

✓ If you leave on the headlights or radio and wake to discover a dead battery, don't automatically assume you need a new one. The battery may only need to be recharged. And it must be fully recharged before it can be tested to determine if a new battery is needed.

A load tester

✓ A **load tester** completes the examination of a fully charged battery. It demands that the battery provide the electrical current necessary to start the car under the simulated conditions of a cold day—the battery's toughest job. If the battery can't generate 9.6 volts at 0° F (-18° C) for 15 seconds it should be replaced.

✓ Periodically check the electrolyte level of a conventional battery by removing the plastic protective covers. The solution inside should reach the bottom of the plastic filler necks. If it doesn't, add distilled water.

CHECK THE EYE

On a "maintenance-free" battery, you can peer at the built-in charge indicator, often called an "eye." If the eye is lit up, your battery is sufficiently charged; if it's dark, it must be charged before testing.

On a conventional battery, your service technician will use a hydrometer (a device that looks like a turkey baster) to determine the general health of the battery.

Money-Saving Tip

The cost of scheduled service varies depending on the tests, adjustments, and repairs that are needed; the make, model, and year of the car; and even the area of the country in which you live. Always call all a few places to be sure that the price you are quoted for service is fair. And be sure you know exactly what is included in each quote you get.

Note: While most batteries today are maintenance-free, it's a good idea to have it professionally tested once a year.

✓ Replace your battery with one of the same size and same (or higher) rating. Charts are available wherever batteries are sold to help you decide which size is right for your car. Do not buy a battery that is rated lower than your owner's manual recommends, or lower than the original battery.

✓ If you have recently installed electronic accessories, such as a cellular telephone or an alarm system, consider upgrading to a higher-rated battery when it comes time to replace your old battery.

✓ When shopping for a new battery, consider the number of years you expect to keep your car. If you're planning on selling your car in six months, think twice before buying a 60-month battery.

✓ Inspect the following starting, charging, and ignition components—as well as any others listed in your owner's manual—once a year, or whenever your owner's manual recommends. Fall, before the onset of cold weather, is a good time for the inspections.

Warning!

Do not smoke near a battery or expose it to an open flame of any kind. Batteries contain explosive gases.

1. Inspect and clean battery terminals.
2. Inspect battery cables and wires.
3. Clean, adjust, or replace spark plugs as needed.
4. Inspect distributor if applicable.
5. Inspect belts for proper tension and replace brittle, flaky, or cracked belts.

✓ Advances in technology are to thank for some newer vehicles that do not require their first scheduled service for 100,000 miles (160,000 kilometers)! These vehicles still require fluid changes and periodic inspections. See your owner's manual for specifics.

Troubleshooting the Ignition and Charging Systems

Possible causes

Symptoms

Symptoms	Shift selector not in park	Faulty starter/solenoid	Battery dirty, discharged, worn out	Loose broken wiring, cables, connections	Faulty neutral safety or ignition switch	Spark plugs, dirty, worn or incorrect gap	Faulty distributor, rotor, coil, ignition wires	Faulty alternator, voltage regulator	Slipping belt	Computer-related	Incorrect timing
No start / hard start (starter works)				●	●	●	●			●	●
No start (starter doesn't work)*	●	●	●	●	●			●	●		
"Check engine" light on				●						●	
Engine runs rough at idle				●		●	●			●	●
Engine runs rough at highway speeds				●		●	●			●	●
Engine stalls or hesitates						●	●			●	●
Engine surges						●					●
Engine lacks power				●		●	●				●
Battery frequently discharges*		●	●					●	●		
Alternator light on			●					●	●		

*Check battery terminals first. Dirt and/or corrosion are often the problem.

4
The Engine

This chapter explains how the engine works and why it sometimes doesn't. It offers specific advice on how to maintain your car's engine, and, if repairs are necessary, what you can do to keep the repair bill somewhere below the national deficit and more in the range of a fast-food dinner for a family of four. ❖

Think of the engine as your car's stomach. Just as your stomach transforms food into energy (with the help of digestive juices), so does your car's engine convert its diet of air and fuel into energy.

STOMACH

The engine

❖

How the Engine Works

The engine takes the chemical energy available in its air-and-fuel diet and, with the help of the spark, converts it into the mechanical energy or motion of its pistons. This motion is then transferred through a series of metal rods to the wheels.

The expanded gases that result from the explosions

The energy of the pistons is transferred through a series of metal rods to the wheels.

❖

would drive a piston right out the bottom of the engine were it not firmly attached to the turning crankshaft. Good thing, too, or we'd be forever stopping to pick them up off the pavement, making progress slow and very expensive.

This impressive transfer of power is what cars are all about: the grand finale, the *pièce de résistance*, and so on.

Engine Layouts

All gasoline engines have certain things in common: Round metal plugs called pistons move up and down as a result of explosions that take place inside smooth round holes called cylinders, which are cut into a hunk of solid metal aptly named the **engine block**. Got that? Good. It's the basis for all knowledge about the engine.

Engines come in a variety of shapes and sizes. The three most common engine layouts as seen on the following page are 1) four or more cylinders "in-line" (in a row), attached to the crankshaft, 2) six cylinders in two rows of three, joined to the crankshaft in a V formation, and 3) eight cylinders arranged in two rows of four, also in V formation.

The heat of the internal explosions causes the pistons and cylinders to expand at different rates. If a piston

In-line 4 cylinder   **V-6 cylinder**   **V-8 cylinder**

❖

were machined to the exact size of the cylinder, there wouldn't be enough room when it expanded for it to move at the breathtaking speed it does. Space must be provided to allow for the expansion, but space would allow gases to escape from the cylinders and reduce compression and power. What to do? Surround the piston by a thin metal ring that expands into the combustion chamber, sealing it and scraping excess oil from the cylinder walls. These rings permit movement, but keep gases from escaping because they act as a seal once the engine heats up.

The Valves

Most of the valve train components are located in a separate metal casing placed over the engine block called the **engine head**. A thin piece of tough material, the **head gasket**, seals the opening where the engine block and head meet.

Located over the top of each cylinder, you will see two objects that look like upside-down golf tees—the **valves**. These valves are actually one-way doors, similar to the valves in your heart, which allow blood to flow in only one direction. Each cylinder has a minimum of two valves: an **intake valve** and an **exhaust valve**.

PISTON RING

Each piston is surrounded by thin metal rings that help to ensure compression and power by sealing in gases.

SPARK PLUG

VALVE GUIDE

EXHAUST PORT

INTAKE PORT

COMBUSTION
CHAMBER

VALVE SEAT

PISTON

Valves in the engine act like the valves in your heart. They are one-way doors that regulate the flow of air and fuel into and out of the cylinders.

❖

The intake valve opens to let the unburned fuel mixture into the upper area of the cylinders, the **combustion chamber**, where the air/fuel mixture will be burned. The valve closes tightly after the fuel mixture is admitted and while it is burning. The exhaust valve opens to permit the burned gases to exit after each burning, thus making room for a new air/fuel mixture to enter once again, via the intake valve.

The valves are attached to the **camshaft**, a round metal bar that gets its name from its metal bumps, or lobes, called **cams**. The camshaft is linked to the crankshaft by a **timing chain**, or **timing belt**. Because these two bars—the crankshaft and the camshaft—are attached to one another, when one turns, so does the other. As the camshaft turns, its lobes push against the valves, forcing them to open and close.

HEAD

HEAD
GASKET

CYLINDERS

BLOCK

Most of the valve components are located in a metal casing called the head. A piece of tough material called the head gasket seals the two surfaces.

❖

Valves never work solo. Depending on the specific design of the engine, hundreds of other parts, lumped under the heading **valve train**, help the valves open and close.

There are several different ways that valve trains can be designed. In a pushrod engine, the camshaft is positioned down in the engine block and connected to the valves by a series of components. These include **springs**, **rocker arms**, **pushrods**, and **tappets**. (An engine that has more than one camshaft—one for intake valves and one for exhaust valves—is called a **dual** or **double overhead cam** engine.)

Alternatively, the camshaft may sit directly over the valves. This popular design is referred to as an **overhead**

Common Valve Train Layouts

A. Pushrod engine　　　　**B. Overhead cam engine**

❖

cam engine. Since there are fewer parts connecting the camshaft to the valves, the engine can often run at higher speeds and produce more power than a similarly sized pushrod engine. With either design, smooth engine performance depends on many small but important parts working in harmony with each other.

The Four Strokes of an Engine

Each movement of a piston, up or down, is called a **stroke**. It takes four strokes to produce power. Let's track the path of just one piston, piston number two, as it plays its part. Each of the other pistons will be doing the same thing, but at a different time.

On stroke 1, the **intake stroke**, the piston moves downward because it is attached to the crankshaft. On cue, the intake valve begins to open. The piston now acts like a big straw drawing the air/fuel mixture in behind it. *Whoosh*. When the cylinder is filled with vapor, the valve closes. The combustion chamber is now sealed.

On stroke 2, the **compression stroke**, the piston moves back up and compresses the fuel mixture into a small space at the top.

On stroke 3, the **power stroke**, the spark is delivered. The compressed air/fuel mixture explodes with the force of many sticks of dynamite—*Kablam!* The heated gases

1. INTAKE   2. COMPRESSION   3. POWER   4. EXHAUST

that result from the explosion expand and push the piston down violently.

During stroke 4, the **exhaust stroke**, which takes place after the explosion, the piston once again rises (this time because the piston next door has just fired, causing the crankshaft to turn again), and another valve, an exhaust valve, opens to expel the hot used gases.

The piston now acts like a reusable bullet. Its powerful and violent up-and-down motion happens over and over again—as many as 100 times per second! Within a fraction of a second, all the pistons are going up and down at the same amazing speed, but at different times, to reduce the vibration that would occur if they were all to ignite at once. The valves may open and close 100,000 times in an hour!

It takes four movements of the piston to turn the crankshaft two revolutions. The crankshaft must turn at

To return to the analogy of the bicyclist to the pistons: those legs just went from a smooth, slow pedal to a blur!

❖

a minimum number of revolutions per minute (rpms) to continue the self-perpetuating motion responsible for producing the turning power of the engine, or **torque**; otherwise, the engine would stall.

Timing

Fred Astaire and Ginger Rogers had it. All successful dancers have it. So do engines that run well. *Timing* is coordination. It is more than one person or part acting in unison to create a desired result.

To accomplish this model of performance, correct timing or coordination must take place among the hundreds of engine components that create, combine, compress, and explode the engine's air/fuel/spark diet. Each component acts like a dancer in a chorus line. If one dancer is a second late in the execution of a step, the entire performance will suffer, and the audience will not be pleased. In a chorus line, everyone must work together for a smooth effect.

The same is true for your car's engine. All the components must work together if the performance is to be smooth and error-free. That your engine—a conglomeration of hundreds of moving parts—performs as smoothly as it does most of the time is perhaps more surprising than that it occasionally stumbles.

As Fred and Ginger knew, the key to a flawless performance is timing.

❖

It is timing that coordinates this mass of movement among the engine's numerous parts, thus ensuring maximum **compression**, which results in maximum engine power and fuel efficiency. The intake valve should open so that a maximum amount of the unburned air/fuel mixture reaches the combustion chamber before compression takes place. The exhaust valve should then open so that a maximum amount of burned gases leaves the chamber immediately after ignition takes place.

The spark reaches the spark plug at the correct moment—just before the piston reaches the top of the cylinder, having thoroughly compressed the air/fuel mixture. That moment in time is called **"Top Dead Center"** in garage-ese.

If the spark plug ignites the air/fuel mixture at any other time (for example, when the piston has already begun to descend), the piston will not travel as far and the engine will not produce as much power. Power is also lost if the valves open at the incorrect time; for example, during the power stroke.

The Computer

On today's cars, the on-board computer that is in charge of fuel delivery and ignition also controls timing and combustion. The computer analyzes the information it receives from many different sensors about the delivery of the spark, the movement of the crankshaft, and the opening and closing of the valves. It continually readjusts their activity for maximum power and efficiency.

The Power Play

Designing engines that produce more power while maintaining good fuel economy has always been one of automotive engineering's primary goals. Simply enlarging the combustion chambers of most small engines

The automotive computer controls timing and combustion.

Frequently asked questions

Q What is the difference between a diesel and a gasoline engine?

A The **diesel engine** is similar in many ways to a **gasoline engine** except that the fuel is ignited simply by the heat of the compressed air, not by a spark plug. Compressing air makes it hotter. In diesel engines, the air is compressed so tightly that it becomes red-hot. Fuel is injected into the cylinder by fuel injectors, then compressed, and the super hot air causes it to explode. What happens to the pistons after that is similar to what happens in gasoline engines. Diesel engines are traditionally more fuel-efficient than their gasoline cousins and able to operate on less expensive diesel fuel. The trade-offs are a heavier engine and a distinct intolerance for even small amounts of water in the fuel delivery system.

The diesel engine

(increasing their **displacement**) provides more power, but it often increases the engine's vibration and sacrifices fuel economy. A desirable alternative is to keep the cylinder the same size and enable it to "eat" its air/fuel diet more quickly. Among the ways to accomplish this are adding valves, **superchargers**, or **turbochargers**.

Multi-valve Engines

Multi-valve engines are those with more than two valves per cylinder. The more air and fuel that enters the cylinders, the greater the explosion. The result is more power without sacrificing good gas economy. The advantages, however, are most noticeable when you accelerate hard, and less noticeable at slower speeds.

Multi-valve engines allow more air into the cylinders.

Superchargers and Turbochargers

Most engines are **normally aspirated**, that is, they draw the air/fuel mixture into the combustion chambers without assistance. As the piston moves downward in the chamber, it creates a **vacuum** behind it into which the air/fuel mixture is drawn. It works like a big straw. To get more power out of a normally aspirated engine, it is necessary to force it to breathe more air and burn more fuel.

Superchargers and turbochargers are pumps that force more air and fuel into the combustion chambers of an engine, forcing them to burn more fuel and produce more power. A supercharger differs from a turbocharger primarily in the method it uses to get additional air and fuel into the combustion chambers.

A supercharger is driven by a belt, which works off the power of the engine. Consequently, it uses some power to provide other power.

Instead of a belt, a turbocharger uses a device called a **turbine**. A turbine is a machine with two sets of blades which spin in oil. The pump is placed in the path of the exhaust gases. Those hot gases turn one blade of the turbine, and that turns the other blade. This forces some of

Superchargers and turbochargers force more air into the cylinders.

the exhaust gases back into the engine. Some of the heat that would normally go out the tailpipe as total waste is now used to generate additional power. Because it takes a second for the exhaust gases to be burned, there is a short delay, called a *lag*, in getting the extra boost to the engine.

Intercoolers and Tuned Intake Manifolds

Superchargers and turbochargers can produce even more power when they are equipped with an **intercooler**. This device, as its name suggests, cools air. Cooler air molecules allow more air molecules to be packed into the combustion chamber and burned for more power. A properly designed intercooler can increase power by 10 percent.

Another way of adding power is to redesign the steel

A tuned intake manifold makes a supercharger or turbocharger even more powerful.

Frequently asked questions

Q What can happen when a car's engine overheats?

A Your engine generates enough heat to melt ordinary steel. If too much heat accumulates, it will damage the engine. The heat can be so intense that it warps or twists the metal cylinder head. It may also burn away the layer of insulation called the head gasket, located between the head and the block. A warped or cracked cylinder head or a blown head gasket will permit the hot combustion gases to escape, resulting in a lack of power and potentially serious engine damage. As if that weren't enough, internal parts, such as pistons and their connecting rods, can warp or break. Even the engine block can crack. Or the worst possible case? The engine can seize—the pistons actually melt into the cylinder walls—never to move again.

tubes that carry the air/fuel mixture to and from the engine (the **intake manifold**) and the exhaust gases away from it (the **exhaust manifold**). Redesigning the manifolds makes the cylinder available for a fresh air/fuel mixture quicker. Both of these methods increase the engine's efficiency and generate more power.

Making your car go the distance
The Engine

Following the schedule of service in your owner's manual will help keep your engine in good working order. Here are some other tips to make your engine last.

 Oil changes are the most important and should be the most frequently performed preventive maintenance. More than anything else you do for your vehicle, regularly changing the oil will extend the serviceable life of your engine. (See chapter 8 for more about oil.)

Money-Saving Tip

Have your timing belt or chain inspected and changed whenever your manufacturer recommends. If a timing belt breaks, it can act like a grenade inside an engine. In seconds it can severely damage valves and even pistons, resulting in expensive repairs to remedy the damage.

✓ Always give your vehicle a minute or two to warm up before driving off. It takes that long for the oil to reach and separate the hundreds of finely machined parts inside the engine.

✓ Before any internal engine work is done, make sure that the fuel and ignition systems have been inspected and adjusted to manufacturer's specifications. Internal engine repair is labor intensive and extremely expensive, so get a written estimate before okaying work. You may also want a second opinion.

✓ If any portion of your engine needs to be rebuilt, be sure the repair shop uses factory-rebuilt and warranted equipment for the replacement parts.

✓ Valves, **valve guides** and seats, rings, and other internal parts wear over time, resulting in a loss of power and an increase in oil consumption. You may have to replace worn internal parts with new ones.

Troubleshooting the Engine

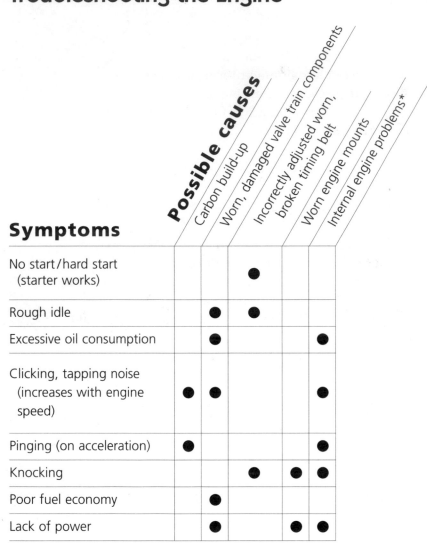

Symptoms	Carbon build-up	Worn, damaged valve train components	Incorrectly adjusted worn, broken timing belt	Worn engine mounts	Internal engine problems*
No start/hard start (starter works)			●		
Rough idle		●	●		
Excessive oil consumption		●			●
Clicking, tapping noise (increases with engine speed)	●	●			●
Pinging (on acceleration)	●				●
Knocking			●	●	●
Poor fuel economy		●			
Lack of power		●		●	●

*Before beginning internal engine diagnosis and repair, a technician should thoroughly inspect ignition, fuel, emission controls, and computerized elements.

5
The Exhaust System and Emission Controls

Proper maintenance of the exhaust and emissions systems is important for the environment, as well as for your safety. This chapter explains how the exhaust and emission control systems work and how you can save money by taking advantage of a special warranty, should you need repairs to these systems. ❖

The exhaust system

❖

Like the human body, cars generate waste, and they must have a way to remove those waste products from their systems in order to remain healthy. The **exhaust system** and emission controls are analogous to the body's intestines. They draw the waste products of combustion, hot exhaust gases, away from the engine and into the atmosphere.

INTESTINES

The exhaust system and emission controls are analogous to the human body's intestines.

These automobile waste products contribute to air pollution. The primary offenders are hydrocarbons, nitrogen oxides, and carbon monoxide. Hydrocarbons and nitrogen oxides are visible in the form of brown clouds that hang over many of our cities—smog. Carbon monoxide, while invisible, is believed to be partly responsible for the attack on the earth's ozone layer.

The exhaust system is made up of a series of metal components that are welded together to route burned gases away from the engine and into the atmosphere.

❖

How the Exhaust System Works

The exhaust system begins at the exhaust manifold, a set of steel pipes that are attached to the engine. Combustion gases that have escaped through the exhaust valves collect in the manifold after burning. These gases are pushed along by the pressure of the incoming gases, until they flow into one or more steel pipes, the **headpipe(s)**.

From the headpipe, the gases go to the **catalytic converter**, a device that looks like a large muffler and contains precious metals that cause a chemical reaction. These metals turn carbon monoxide and hydrocarbons into harmless substances such as water and carbon dioxide.

Frequently asked questions

Q Why does my car smell like rotten eggs?

A The catalytic converter is often responsible for this odor. It occurs as a result of the burning of sulfur present in gasoline. It's normal for this odor to occur occasionally, but it can be a warning sign of a clogged or defective system. Try switching brands of gasoline. If that doesn't help, check with your dealer to see if there is a factory fix, and ask if the cost is covered by warranty.

From the converter, gases go on to the **muffler**, an oblong metal noise-catcher that absorbs much of the sound that combustion creates by routing sound waves through its perforated pipes. The remaining gases may reach the atmosphere by way of the final exhaust pipe, the **tailpipe**, or they may pass through another sound-reducing device called a **resonator**. What reaches the atmosphere is our car's contribution to the planet: pollution.

The Emission Controls System

Since the early 1960s, environmental protection laws have attempted to reduce pollutants by requiring the use of certain exhaust and emission control devices that control the amount of pollutants (gases and particulates) engines produce. To describe in depth the emission control components found on most cars today, we would need another book of this size. What is important to know is that emission control components are instrumental in reducing pollution. Unfortunately, they also affect the performance of your car's engine.

Here is a list of some of the major devices and a brief description of how they work. (Your car may have a few or many of these emission control devices, as well as additional devices not listed here.)

The major emission control components

❖

The **exhaust gas recirculation (EGR) system** recirculates exhaust gases back to the engine, where they are burned again.

The **exhaust gas conversion** system includes the catalytic converter and *oxygen sensor*.

The **evaporative emission control (EEC) system** traps vapors from the fuel system and redirects them to the engine, where they are stored in a charcoal canister. Instead of being released into the atmosphere, these fumes are burned in the engine when the engine is restarted.

The **positive crankcase ventilation (PCV) system** picks up "blow-by gases" that have escaped into the crankcase from the combustion chambers and returns them to the engine to be burned.

The **pre-heated-air-intake system** uses hot exhaust gases to maintain the flow of warm air into the engine.

Money-Saving Tip

Special Federal Emissions Warranty

If your emission control system fails because of a defective part, whether or not the part failure causes your car's emissions to exceed federal emission standards, the manufacturer is required by federal law to pay for the repairs for the first five years or 50,000 miles (80,000 kilometers).

Warning!
A faulty exhaust system can allow harmful gases into the passenger compartment, resulting in possible carbon monoxide poisoning. An annual inspection by a service professional is a must.

This allows for a more combustible mixture that requires less fuel and burns more completely.

Many of the ignition and fuel delivery components on both fuel-injected and carburetor models have been developed to control emissions. On fuel-injected systems, these devices include the fuel injectors and the computer. On carburetor models, the mixture control unit, the electronic choke, and the thermostatic air cleaner were developed to help curb emissions.

Making your car go the distance
Exhaust and Emission Controls Systems

The exhaust and emissions systems should be checked regularly to ensure that they are operating correctly. Here are some other items to be aware of.

✓ Rattles, roars, knocks, buzzes, and chatters coming from under the car, particularly those that are especially noticeable at idle, are very often the result of loose parts, fasteners, or hangers that cause the metal components to come in contact with the bottom of the car. Many times, simply retightening the exhaust components will set the system right.

Many states require vehicles to pass an emissions standards test before new tags will be issued.

❖

✓ If your muffler needs replacement and you are told that it is a one-piece assembly (meaning you get to buy the exhaust pipe as well as the muffler, even though yours might be in good shape), ask if there is an adapter available so that the new muffler can be fitted to your old exhaust pipe.

✓ Always read the guarantee for muffler replacement carefully, and file it and the bill in a safe place.

✓ In many places government regulations require vehicles to pass an emission standards test. Having your vehicle serviced regularly will help it to pass even the most rigorous local inspection programs.

Troubleshooting the Exhaust System and Emission Controls

Symptoms	Loose or damaged exhaust components	Restricted, bent exhaust components	Faulty catalytic converter	Inoperative PCV valve	Inoperative EGR system	Inoperative EEC system
Possible causes						
Hard start				●		
Rough idle			●	●	●	
Hesitation/stalling			●	●		
Hesitation/cold						●
Surging				●		
Lack of power		●	●	●		
Pinging/knocking					●	●
Engine overheats		●	●			
Rattling/humming/ buzzing sound	●		●			
Loud exhaust	●					

6
The Electrical System

Without the electrical network, your vehicle's "nervous system," none of the car's other systems can function. In this chapter, you'll learn why electrical problems occur, and how to handle the simpler repairs while avoiding paying too much for the not-so-simple repairs. ❖

The electrical system

❖

Your car's electrical system can be compared to the human body's nervous system.

The electrical system of your car acts like the nervous system in your body. In your body, important messages are passed through nerve cells in the form of tiny electrical currents. In your car, messages are passed through metal wires in the form of not-so-tiny electrical currents. Automotive messages are converted into power for the ignition, computers, lights, and accessories.

Just as the body has more than one nervous system—one for the muscles and another that controls such functions as sweating—so, too, do cars. Today's cars have at least two electrical systems, sometimes more. The central electrical system controls the ignition, lights, and accessories, while a second system controls the engine management computer. There may also be a third system, one to control such devices as electronic brakes. For more about brakes, see chapter 12.

How the Electrical System Works

Electricity begins and ends at the battery. That's where electrical current rests when the engine is not running. When the engine is turned on, current leaves the battery to provide electricity for the ignition, lights, and accessories. Electrical currents, though, are essentially homebodies; they will not leave the battery unless they are assured of a return ticket home. In electrical terms, that return ticket is called a **circuit**, or return loop.

It's the same in your home. Current will not flow without a return loop. In your home, a metal wire takes the current to its destination and returns it to its point of origin by way of a second metal wire. With lots of storage space hidden behind the walls of your home, this system works great. In your car, a wiring system that provided a second return wire for each light and accessory would look like a spaghetti factory gone berserk. Your car's frame, being made of metal, makes a great oversized return wire. It is the frame of the car that provides the return loop for the electrical current and

Electrical current will not flow unless there is a return loop.

WIRE GROUNDED
TO CAR BODY

The metal frame of the car acts as an oversized return wire and provides the return loop for electrical current. This is referred to as grounding.

completes the circuit. This is referred to as **grounding**. Any cable, strap, metal bolt, or mount that connects an electrical component to the frame is called a ground.

Switches, Relays, Fuses, Fusible Links, and Circuit Breakers

Each return loop or circuit has a **switch** that acts like a drawbridge. When the drawbridge is lowered, the circuit is complete and the current can move or flow; when the drawbridge is up, the circuit is incomplete and the current cannot flow. For example, when you turn on the headlights for night driving, a switch lowers the drawbridge for that light's circuit, the circuit is complete, and current flows to the headlights.

Relays are backup safety switches that are used on circuits with particularly strong electrical current; for example, the ignition, the windshield wiper motor, and the horn.

Just as any metal or plastic device can malfunction, so can switches and relays. A relay can simply stop working, and current will not flow to the accessory in its charge. A switch can become stuck in the "on" position, completing the circuit so there is current constantly

SWITCH

Switches and relays act like drawbridges: they allow electrical current to move across them only when they're lowered.

going to the light or accessory—even when you assume it's not. Even if the accessory or light doesn't use a lot of current, it doesn't take long before the reserve current of the battery is completely used up—and you have a dead battery on your hands. *Note:* Recharging the battery and replacing the switch will usually solve the problem.

Fuses, fusible links, and circuit breakers guard the electrical system from fires resulting from overheating due to excessive electricity. Most accessories have fuses that are wires contained within plastic or glass tubes. If too much voltage surges through a circuit and causes it to get too hot, the wire element in the fuse melts or "blows." Consequently, there is a gap of air between the wires that carry the current. Air is an insulator, not a conductor of current; it prevents the passage of electricity. So when a fuse blows, the flow of current is interrupted.

Fusible links accomplish the same thing as fuses, but rather than being enclosed in glass or plastic and placed

MULTI-WIRING
CONNECTOR
PRINTED
CIRCUIT BOARD

BULB MOUNTING
HOLE
PLATED
WIRING

Printed circuits of metal bonded onto plastic are often used behind the dashboard to reduce the amount of wiring.

together in a box, they are thinner pieces of wire located at strategic points in the wiring. If there is a surge of current, the thinner wire melts and the circuit is broken.

Circuit breakers are spring-loaded devices that retract when they receive a current surge. To be without the use of an accessory because a fuse, fusible link, or circuit breaker has melted or sprung may be very inconvenient temporarily, but it sure beats the alternative—a fire.

Warning! If you detect the odor of burning rubber or plastic while driving, it could be the wiring insulation burning away from, or rubbing against, the metal of the body. This is a warning to be heeded! Have the electrical system inspected as soon as possible. It could be the start of an electrical fire.

A short is a circuit that returns to the battery before reaching its destination.

What Can Go Wrong?

Electrical problems invariably result from the inability of electrical current to get from the battery to the component and back to the battery again. This inability to return home is usually the result of a **short** or an **open**.

A short is a circuit that is accidentally shortened; it forces the current to return to its source before it reaches its destination (a headlight, for example, or the horn). A short often is the result of the insulating material around the wire wearing away. Stripped of its insulation, the wire can touch against the metal of the car, and the current can return home via the quickest and easiest path, the frame.

One of the most common opens occurs when dirt restricts the movement of current where two wires meet.

A short often causes a fuse to blow. If a fuse is replaced and it blows again immediately, it could be that the vibration of the car traveling along the road is causing the intermittent contact of a wire with the car's metal frame. If it happens often and can't be traced, the only answer is to replace the wiring in that circuit.

An open circuit can also cause the flow of current to be interrupted. If a wire is broken or frayed in such a way that air comes between the two pieces of wire, the air acts as an insulator, not a conductor, and interrupts the flow of current. An open circuit can occur as a result of a broken wire, a bad switch, a burned-out bulb, a malfunctioning motor, or a faulty connection. One of the most common opens occurs when dirt or corrosion collects where two wires connect. The dirt creates resistance and restricts the movement of the current. Cleaning or replacing the connector should correct the problem.

*The **starting circuit** consists of the battery, ignition switch, starter, starter switch, wires, and frame.*
*The **charging circuit** consists of the battery, alternator, voltage regulator, wires, and frame.*
*The **ignition circuit** consists of the battery, ignition switch, coil, distributor, spark plugs, and computer.*
*The **accessory circuit** consists of the battery, lights, dash instruments, windshield wiper, horn, and any other power devices, including seats, windows, or antenna.*

Starting, Charging, and Ignition Circuits

Cars have four basic circuits, as shown in the illustration on the previous page. Since we've already discussed the starting, charging, and ignition systems in chapters 3 and 4, the rest of this chapter will concentrate on accessories.

Lights

The light system includes brake lights, headlights, side markers, directional lights, and hazard lights, which are all mandatory on today's cars. Most lights operate in a similar manner: wires run through and into a bulb that is attached to a tungsten filament, a piece of fine wire. Current flows to the bulb through the wire and the socket, and then on to the filament. The current causes tiny particles in the filament to heat up, sending out showers of glowing sparks. This glow is called incandescence. A bulb can contain more than one filament, as do taillights, stoplights, and some headlights.

Dashboard Instrumentation

The instrumentation circuit is made up of gauges and warning lights. When you turn on the car, all the dashboard lights should go on, then go out immediately afterward.

Dashboard instrumentation

A **sending unit** or sensor relays information to the gauges or computer about the volume, temperature, and pressure of the gasoline, oil, and coolant, among other things.

Turn Signals

Today's directionals are operated by a **flasher unit**. That's a switch that turns the directional bulbs on and off 60 to 120 times per minute; it also activates the flashing emergency hazard lights.

Windshield Wipers

The windshield wipers are run by a small electrical motor that has a connecting arm to the wiper arms. Wiper motors have a fuse and at least one, and sometimes two, switches. The first switch signals the wipers to stop, while the second switch, called the wiper park switch, allows the wiper arms to return to their original position after you turn them off.

LINKAGE

WIPER MOTOR

The Horn

Depressing the horn button sends an electrical current to a magnet, causing a vibration that results in an audible signal.

Electrical System

Modern wiring systems, despite their complexity, cause relatively few problems and usually require little attention. Here are a few tips to keep the system operating smoothly.

✓ Get a friend to help you inspect all of your car's lights, directionals, and warning signals monthly to be sure they are working properly. Check your owner's manual for the correct procedure for changing the bulbs in your car.

Warning!
Touching a halogen bulb—such as those used in headlights—with your bare hands will destroy it. Always wear gloves.

Check your car's lights, directionals, and warning signals monthly to be sure they are working properly.

❖

✓ Make sure your car's horn is working correctly by giving it a blast on a regular basis.

✓ Inspect windshield wiper blades whenever you clean your windshield. Replace blades at least once a year or when they become cracked or brittle, or smear the windshield. If you buy from an auto parts store, be sure the parts people show you exactly how to install the new ones.

✓ If you live in an area with severe winters, switch to winter blades before the season's first snowfall. And

Worn, cracked, or dirty windshield wiper blades can be a real safety hazard.

❖

be sure to clean off heavy deposits of snow and free frozen or stuck wiper blades before turning on the car.

✓ If your windshield wipers stop working, it could be just a blown fuse, not a failed motor. Before the motor is replaced, be sure the fuse is okay.

✓ All cars have at least one fuse box, and many have more than one. To find the fuse box in your car, look in your owner's manual or have your service provider show you.

✓ Be sure you carry extra fuses that are the correct size as indicated in your owner's manual.

✓ Get in the habit of turning off all electrical devices when you park the car.

Consult your owner's manual for the location of the fuse box(es) in your car.

Troubleshooting the Electrical System

Possible causes

Symptoms	Faulty switch	Battery discharged, worn out	Bulb, contact at bulb socket	Fuse*	Fusible link, circuit breaker switch relay	Wiring, ground, connection	Voltage regulator	Instrument voltage regulator	Gauge, sending unit sensor	Flasher unit, turn signal
Headlights dim	●	●	●		●	●				
Headlights don't work	●		●	●	●	●				
No high or low beam	●		●		●	●				
Bulbs burn out frequently							●			
Turn signals don't work	●		●			●				●
Turn signals flash on one side only	●		●	●		●				
Warning lights or gauges don't work			●			●		●	●	
Power windows or locks don't work	●			●	●	●				
Horn doesn't work				●		●				
Windshield wipers don't work	●			●		●				

*Always check fuses first when troubleshooting any electrical problem.

7
Automotive Computers

Most cars built today have at least one, and usually several, on-board computers. This chapter explains how automotive computers work and why they have changed the nature and cost of auto repairs. You'll learn what you can do to minimize repair costs and what to do if you have an intermittent performance problem. ❖

The automotive computer is the car's "brain." Just as different parts of the brain do different jobs, different parts of the computer serve different functions.

❖

The computer in your car, sometimes called an electronic control module (ECM) or electronic control unit (ECU), is really a computer chip or microprocessor. Similar to the central processing unit in your personal computer, it's an

TOUCH

COLD

WARMTH

PRESSURE

PAIN

SKIN RECEPTORS

The brain and the computer both receive information from different types of receptors.

on-board, whiz-bang electronic brain. And like all brains, it processes information and comes up with answers, making possible the successful completion of many tasks.

Just as different parts of the human brain do different jobs, different parts of the computer serve different functions. The cerebrum controls memory and thinking, for example, and the cerebellum controls the nerves. In a car's "brain," one part controls fuel management and delivery while another is in charge of spark control.

Not only that, your car probably has more than one computer—perhaps as many as three or more. One computer is in charge of engine management, one may control the temperature inside the passenger compartment, and another may be helping you to avoid skids by controlling the brakes and traction.

The human brain and automotive computer both receive information from different types of receptors. The body's receptors give us our senses—taste, smell, and the ability to feel pain, for example. The car's "receptors" are electronic sensors or feelers that record information

CRANKSHAFT
SENSOR

THROTTLE POSITION
SENSOR

COMPUTER CHIP

CORE (INSIDE MANIFOLD)

OXYGEN SENSOR

Computer with sensors

about the speed of the engine (the engine rpm sensor), the temperature of the coolant (coolant sensor), the position of the accelerator pedal (throttle position sensor), and many other factors. This information helps the car to run smoothly and efficiently.

How Computers Work

In order to function properly, your brain relies on the information it receives from your sense organs. Different

How receptors work in humans: Person pets cat with a bad attitude; pain receptors inside the "petter" send signals to direct the muscles to withdraw the hand from the "petee." This solves the problem by taking away the source of the pain.

❖

types of receptors record information about the things you come in contact with in your world. Your skin, for example, has millions of nerve endings that act as pain receptors. If you eat a piece of pizza that is too hot, a pain signal is sent to the brain that says "Ouch! Do something to protect yourself from being burned!"

The automotive equivalent of the body's receptors are sensors—electronic eyes, ears, and nerve endings that record information about the speed of the engine, the temperature and density of the outside air, and much more. With this input, the computer then determines the best air/fuel mixture, how hot the spark should be, and when it should be delivered, what to do to reduce emissions, and hundreds of other pieces of information that help the car to run smoothly and efficiently.

The car's computer works in a similar way. Among the engine computer's sensors is an oxygen sensor, referred to in the automobile industry as the "O_2 sensor." This important device monitors the amount of oxygen left in the stream of exhaust gases leaving the engine. If the O_2 sensor finds that the mixture has too much or too little oxygen, it informs the computer in the form of lightning-fast Morse code. If the computer detects too much

The oxygen sensor monitors the amount of oxygen left in the stream of exhaust gases leaving the engine.

❖

oxygen, for example, it consults a database where alternative air/fuel combinations ideally suited for different driving conditions are stored. Like all computer information, these combinations are stored in memory boxes called cells. Having found the right cell, the computer corrects the air/fuel mixture by instructing the fuel injectors that more fuel is needed. It changes the length of time that the injectors remain open or turns them on more frequently, thus changing the amount of fuel delivered.

A computer may fine-tune the air/fuel mixture as

When automotive sensors don't work, the driver usually notices engine performance problems.

❖

many as ten times a second! That's child's play for this brain, since its electronic signals are traveling at the speed of light: 186,000 miles (299,500 kilometers) per second!

There are, however, limits to the electronic problem-solving system. Just as with your body, if one or more of

Computers are improving the efficiency and safety of our vehicles. In their most recent applications, computers act as radars, warning us to take evasive action if another object gets too close for comfort. Still others can map out the best route to take in order to arrive at a destination without traffic tie-ups.

Although it's not exactly wizardry, computer care is definitely a job for the experts.

❖

your senses were to malfunction, you'd have difficulty operating normally. Likewise, trouble occurs when automotive sensors are damaged by dirt, excessive heat, or vibrations. This can garble the data sent to the computer, or cut it off completely. When this occurs, the driver usually notices engine performance problems, such as hard starting, rough running, power loss, and even stalling. Poor fuel economy and high emissions may also be the result of sensor malfunction. When problems such as these crop up, it's time for a professional to analyze the system.

When Things Go Wrong

Computer care is a job for the experts. Just as you wouldn't want anyone but a trained neurosurgeon to operate on your brain, you shouldn't want anyone but a trained technician to care for your car's brain. A medical doctor can often diagnose a patient's problems by listening to her symptoms and then running a series of specific tests based on those symptoms. In the same way, a service technician with the proper training and test equipment can track down a car's problems and correct them.

Automotive computers monitor their own activity. When a problem is detected, the computer often stores the problem as a number, a "trouble code," in its memory. By connecting an engine analyzer to the on-board computer, a technician can draw data from the analyzer, diagnose the problem, and suggest the most likely causes. The technician may then make a precise adjustment or replace a faulty sensor or other computer component. When the check is run again, the code displayed will indicate that the problem has been corrected, or, if not, the test will be run again and the next likely set of causes reviewed.

Intermittent Problems

But what happens if the problem did not register a trouble code and will not duplicate itself for the benefit of the technician? Just as our teeth seem to stop aching whenever we sit down in the dentist's chair, a car often seems to get better the closer we get to the repair shop. Naturally, if it is an intermittent problem, you will want the technician to road test the car in order to re-create the problem, but even that may not help if the car is unwilling to cooperate.

Diagnostic devices are available which can be installed in a vehicle to detect intermittent problems.

Fortunately, some computers do record intermittent problems. For those that don't, there is equipment available, similar to an airplane's flight recorder, that can be installed on an uncooperative vehicle to detect a sporadic problem. The car can be driven normally until the problem occurs again, when the device will register it. Unfortunately, these devices (actually referred to as "flight recorders" by technicians) are expensive. They will, however, capture that elusive intermittent problem and record it so that the culprit can be identified and remedied. If you are experiencing this type of problem, ask if the shop you are working with has this device. If not, find one that does. The last thing

Frequently asked questions

Q How do I find out if a Technical Service Bulletin (TSB) has been issued for my car's computer problem?

A Ask the dealership nearest you or call the customer service representative's toll-free number listed in your owner's manual. If the TSB involves a safety-related problem, you can contact the National Highway Traffic Safety Administration's office in Washington, D.C. at (202) 366-2768. Some independent repair shops can also access this information by subscribing to a CD-ROM auto database.

you want is to be working with R & R people—mechanics who "Remove and Replace" parts without the slightest idea of what they are doing. Guess who picks up the bill for their ignorance?

Just as you would a doctor, get a second opinion if the cause of your problem is not diagnosed within a reasonable time.

Remember that all computer engine analyzers are not equal. Different shops have very different levels of sensitivity in their diagnostic equipment. Some will respond with such a long list of possible causes that it would take forever to narrow down the real culprit by trial and error. Furthermore, the same equipment can be operated differently. One technician may use the equipment to test only one system, perhaps missing a problem in another system that isn't the likely source but is a possible one.

Sometimes, despite the best efforts of individual and machine, the problem remains elusive. It may be a defect that occurs frequently in a particular model. If so, it may finally be figured out at the manufacturer by some very

Money-Saving Tip

If you are told that your car's computer or one of its sensors is defective, be sure you work with a dealership. In most cases the computer is covered under the manufacturer's warranty, or under the 5-year, 50,000-miles federal emission warranty.

bright technician who specializes in problem-solving. The manufacturer will then issue a Technical Service Bulletin (TSB). If there is no TSB for your problem, the repair shop may have to call in the cavalry, in the form of the manufacturer's technical assistance department, to help them. If the service provider you're using does not have access to this type of technical assistance or isn't able or willing to undertake these additional measures, the likelihood that they will ever get the fix right is, as the mathematicians say, "seriously small."

In fact, if they do get the fix right, it's probably more the result of serendipity than technical know-how. Just as you would with a medical doctor, get a second opinion if the cause of your problem is not diagnosed within a reasonable time. For more on communicating symptoms to your technician, see chapter 14.

Troubleshooting Computers

Due to the diversity and complexity of today's computerized systems, it is not practical to list probable causes of computer problems in a troubleshooting chart. Better to leave this task to the experts.

8
Oil

LIVER
LUNG
HEART
STOMACH
KIDNEY
INTESTINE

This chapter covers the most important (and what should be the most frequent) preventive maintenance chore for your car—checking and changing the oil. It also describes how to choose the right oil for your car and what those numbers (10W-30, etc.) on the oil container mean. Reading this chapter and following its advice will help you to avoid major engine failure. ❖

OIL FILTER
OIL PUMP
OIL PAN

Where oil is stored in your engine

❖

Oil is the lifeblood of your car's engine, and, like the blood that circulates through your body, it must be of a certain quality and quantity to supply all its dependent parts.

Oil Cleans, Cools, and Lubricates

Oil is a jack-of-all-trades. It lubricates, it cleans, and it cools. It is the lifeblood of your car's engine, and, like the blood that circulates through your body, it must be of a certain quality and quantity to supply all of its dependent

OIL GALLEY

THE OIL PUMP IS
LIKE A HEART

OIL FILTER

PAPER FILTER

OIL MOLECULES

The oil system

❖

parts adequately. If the circulation is cut off because the fluid is too thick or too thin, or because a passageway is restricted, or because there is a leak somewhere in the system, it won't be long before damage (often irreparable) is done. Without oil, your engine's a goner. Multi-grade oils have additives that keep oil flowing like cooking oil all year long.

How Oil Works

When the car is not in use, most of the oil sits in a metal oil pan attached to the bottom of the engine. As the ignition key is turned on, an oil pump pressurizes the oil and forces it through a screen. The screen catches large particles of dirt and grit. The oil is then pumped through the regular **oil filter**. The oil filter catches smaller bits of dirt and contaminants, the natural by-products of combustion, and stores them until the filter is changed.

No matter how smooth a metal surface may appear, tiny irregularities exist that can cause friction. Oil separates and coats the metal moving parts so that they can slide smoothly over each other.

From the filter, the oil is pushed through tiny enclosed passageways, or **oil galleys**, that are cut into the engine block. Now the oil moves to the bearings, connecting rods, and inside the cylinder walls, pistons, and valves, where it acts as a lubricant. It separates the metal parts with a thin film of fluid that acts as a slippery cushion. Without this protective coating, the bearings, pistons, valves, and other internal parts would be in direct contact with each other—a destructive situation.

Lubrication

In order for the metal moving parts of the engine to be efficient they have to fit tightly together. But without oil, the tightly fitting surfaces would quickly wear because *metal against metal causes friction, friction causes heat, and heat causes wear.*

At the same time that the oil is acting as a lubricant by separating the moving engine parts, it is providing another benefit as well: it is helping to cool the engine. Since it is a reasonably good conductor of heat, the oil picks up some of the excess heat as it flows around the hot combustion chambers and carries that heat to the oil pan below. This clever design works like clockwork if (1) the oil is at the proper level; (2) the oil is clean and of the correct weight and type; (3) the filter, pump, and other components are working properly; and (4) the passageways are not restricted.

Choosing the Right Oil

Because oil is as essential to an engine's health and well-being as blood is to our body's health, it must perform correctly. It has to flow easily enough to get up inside the cylinder walls and passageways. It must do this very quickly after the engine begins running, otherwise the metal parts will rub against each other without the lubrication they need. *Note:* Most engine wear occurs within the first few moments after the car is started.

OIL FILTER   OIL PUMP

Oil is circulated around each of the cylinders, where it picks up some of the excess heat and carries it to the oil pan below.

In the wintertime oil turns from the consistency of cooking oil to that of honey. During summer, oil thins out to the consistency of vinegar.

How to Read an Oil Can

The information printed on the oil container refers to the viscosity and grade of the oil. Letters such as **API** assure you that the oil meets the warranty standards set by the American Petroleum Institute (API) and the Society of Automotive Engineers (SAE). Numbers such as **10W-30** refer to viscosity, the oil's ability to flow at different temperatures. This ability is indicated by a range, 5 through 50. The smaller the number, the thinner the oil. **W** means that the oil is suitable for use in the winter. Letters such as **SF** refer to the oil's quality. **S** means the oil is suitable for gasoline engines. **C** means it is suitable for diesel engines. High power engines are indicated by a higher letter—SH has better anti-wear additives than SG, for example. **Energy Conserving** means just that: this oil can help improve fuel economy.

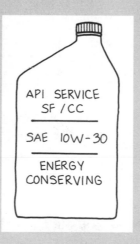

API SERVICE
SF / CC

SAE 10W-30

ENERGY
CONSERVING

With as many types of oil on the market today as there are flavors of ice cream, the task of choosing the right oil can seem daunting; it doesn't have to be.

To coat the internal parts adequately, oil should flow like cooking oil. Oil's consistency, however, changes in response to outside temperatures. Cold temperatures cause the oil to go from the consistency of cooking oil to that of honey. In this honey-like state, the oil might not reach the rapidly moving internal parts in time to separate and protect them. Warm temperatures cause the oil to thin out. It goes from the consistency of cooking oil to that of vinegar. In this state, the oil can't coat and separate the moving parts because it doesn't remain on them long enough. If it's too thick or too thin, the oil can't protect your engine.

For many years, the answer to temperature fluctuations was to change the weight of the oil in summer and in winter. As the temperature dropped, you would change from your car's normal weight oil for your car to

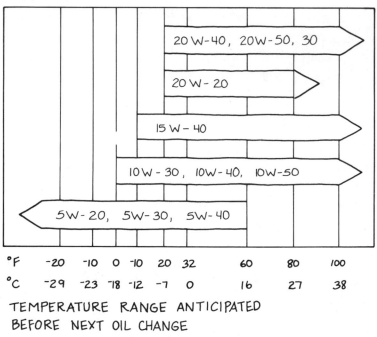

RECOMMENDED SAE   VISCOSITY GRADES

Check your owner's manual for the correct oil weight for your car, and be sure to refer to the temperature range chart. It will tell you whether to change weights based on the season.

a thinner one (from 40 to 30). The smaller the number, the thinner the oil. The thin oil was replaced with a thicker one as the temperature rose.

As petroleum product technology developed, **multi-grade oils** were developed. Additives were included in the oil to extend its working range. For example, additives gave an oil with a weight of 10W-30 the ability to flow freely at more than one temperature range—the 10W meant the oil was suitable for winter (that's what the "W" stands for) and the 30 meant it would also flow well in the summer. Check your owner's manual for the correct weight for your car, and be sure to refer also to the temperature range chart.

In the old days, people in cold climates often didn't drive their cars in the winter because of the great difficulty in starting them. Sometimes they even built a fire under the engine block to warm the engine oil so it would flow more easily. Another common practice was to drain the engine oil into a container and then bring it into the house and set it next to the wood stove, where it would be kept warm and remain thin enough to make starting easier. In the morning, it would be taken back out to the car and poured into the crankcase. What this method lacked in excitement it made up for in messiness.

Specialty Oils

Engine oils were traditionally made by refining or purifying petroleum. Scientists theorize that petroleum is the compressed remains of entire plant and animal civilizations long since buried and preserved in a state of decomposition.

For some years now, petroleum producers have been making engine oils from a synthetic base in a chemist's laboratory. These "designer" oils are able to reach moving parts more quickly than petroleum-based oils. They are especially suitable for extremely cold climates. Their ability to flow at very low temperatures is part of the reason, but they also resist breaking down or "shearing"

Warning!
You may void a new car warranty if you use the wrong oil. Stick with your manufacturer's recommendation.

For some years now, petroleum producers have been making engine oils in the chemist's laboratory.

under hard use. As oil cools and warms in response to changes in engine temperature, it loses both additives and consistency. Synthetics resist breakdown to a greater degree than traditional oils.

Making your car go the distance
Oil Systems

With the rise in popularity of self-serve gas stations, we are required to perform more and more of our own routine maintenance. Smelling like *eau de gasoline* may never come into vogue, but if we ignore these maintenance

How to check your oil

procedures, the consequences may be premature wear of engine parts, resulting in expensive and unnecessary repair bills.

How and When to Check Oil

To check your oil, park on level ground and wait at least five minutes after turning off the engine. Or check the oil when the engine is cold.

1. Pull out the oil dipstick.

2. Wipe it down with a clean cloth.

3. Put the stick back in all the way, as close as possible to the angle at which it came out.

4. Pull it out again, and look at where the oil film lies on the stick in relation to the **add** and **full** lines.

5. If the film is below the **add** line, add a quart (liter) of the oil recommended in your owner's manual. If it is between the **add** and **full** lines, continue to check it regularly.

6. Repeat steps 1 through 5.

Even if your engine oil dipstick has been cleverly disguised by your manufacturer, it's important to find it so you can check the oil every time you add gas, or every other week.

Frequently asked questions

Q What does the word "lube" mean when I have my car's oil changed?

A "Lube" is a carryover from times when cars had many **fittings**, places where metal parts came together and had to be lubricated to prevent friction. Old grease is removed and new grease added. Some early models had as many as 63 fittings that had to be lubricated every time the motorist drove the vehicle! On today's vehicles, most of these fittings are sealed at the factory and no longer require any maintenance.

Money-Saving Tip

Too much oil is also bad for your engine. The oil turns into the consistency of beaten egg whites.

Make sure your oil level is high enough—but not too high. If there is too much oil, the engine seals, which means no oil escapes through the joints and they may burst, leaving you with an oil leak. Too much oil also raises the oil level to the point where the crankshaft actually rests in it. As the crankshaft turns, it whips the oil, adding air to it, just as an eggbeater would. The oil will have the consistency of egg whites: airy. Great for meringues, not good for engines. Airy oil loses its "stickability." It will reach the cylinder walls but it won't stay there. If the dipstick is reading significantly more than full, have it checked by a professional. Have the pan drained to the proper level, if necessary. Your engine will love you for it and live longer.

Just as clogged arteries can cause serious health problems, unburned deposits from the engine eventually thicken the oil and coat the engine's inner parts, causing them to work harder and wear faster.

Changing the Oil and Filter

In order to get the maximum mileage out of your vehicle, have the oil changed every 3,500 miles (5,000 kilometers) or every spring, summer, winter, and fall. Always replace the filter when you have the oil changed.

✓ Consult your owner's manual for the correct weight and quality of oil for your vehicle.

✓ Always ask for the specific oil recommended by your manufacturer. Do not assume the person doing the oil change will know.

✓ Keep track of how much oil your engine uses. It's the change in use that's important. If you notice a sudden change in oil consumption, you should have a professional look at your car.

Warning!

An activated oil gauge or "idiot" light is a screaming, hopping call for help. The light is saying: "Oh driver, there's something happening down here, and I really think you should know about it!" Usually what's happening is that your engine parts are sautéing!

✓ If you are driving a turbocharged or supercharged vehicle, use only a turbo-rated oil. They are specifically designed to handle the tremendous heat that is generated by a turbocharger or supercharger (see chapter 4 for more about superchargers). The carbon deposits that are formed while the engine cools down may coat the bearings and cause them to wear away at a fast and expensive rate. The extra protection of turbo-rated oils is necessary and well worth the additional cost.

Troubleshooting the Oil System

Symptoms	Low oil, wrong weight, diluted oil	Loose or leaking oil filter cap	Oil leaking externally**	Burning internally***	Faulty oil pressure sending switch, sensor, wiring	Broken or worn oil pump	Malfunctioning warning light or gauge	Malfunctioning PCV valve
Oil warning light on, or no pressure on gauge*	●				●	●	●	
Oil fumes/burning smell		●	●					
Excess oil consumption		●	●	●				●
Engine leaks oil			●					●
Clicking/tapping noise	●							
Engine hesitates		●						

*Danger! Don't drive the car!
**Could be leaking by loose oil filter, drain plug, gaskets, front or rear engine seal, worn valve components, rings or pistons or other engine parts
***Even the most difficult-to-find leaks can be detected with the use of a "black light" and special dye.

9
The Cooling, Heating, and Air Conditioning Systems

Cooling system failures remain one of the major causes of highway breakdowns. In this chapter you'll learn how to keep your engine (and yourself) from overheating. You will also learn a few simple preventive maintenance steps that will help you to avoid the costly replacement of expensive cooling, heating, and air conditioning components. ❖

The cooling, heating, and air conditioning systems

❖

The Engine Cooling System

Today's engines work harder and handle greater heat than ever before. The explosions taking place inside the engine produce temperatures in excess of 2,500° F

Just as the human body has sweat glands to help maintain the correct body temperature, the cooling system in a car's engine maintains the correct engine temperature range. It's your car's way of sweating.

Today's engines produce enough heat to warm a three-bedroom house.

(1,500° C)—enough heat to melt ordinary steel. That's also enough heat to warm a three-bedroom house on a freezing cold day. What you have under the hood of your car is a mini Dante's inferno.

Just as your body has an ideal temperature range, so does your car. Both are equipped with temperature control systems. When your body gets too hot, temperature sensors in your brain advise the body to sweat and the blood vessels to widen. More heat from the body passes through the skin into the air—that's how the body cools itself. If your body temperature rises significantly for a prolonged period of time, whether as a consequence of a fever or of sitting in the hot sun without a hat, damage may result—even death. Similarly, if the temperature of an engine rises beyond a certain point for a significant time, there is a high risk of damaging or destroying the engine.

Most cars are water-cooled. For these the cooling system depends on the flow of liquid called **coolant** (more about what coolant is later on) in and around the engine. There are, however, a few air-cooled engines, which depend on the flow of air in and around the engine, as well as on the cooling properties of oil. The most popular and efficient application of the air-cooled engine was in the Volkswagen Beetle.

How the Cooling System Works

The cooling system works in the following way:

1. A liquid called coolant is stored in the radiator, which consists of a metal tank and many narrow metal tubes which make up the **core**. A radiator cap seals the system and puts it under 14 to 18 pounds of pressure per square inch (PSI).

2. When the engine is running, a water pump that is powered by a belt attached to the engine draws coolant out of the radiator and into the engine compartment through a radiator hose. From there, it circulates through tiny copper-lined passageways that make up the engine's **water jacket**. As the coolant travels through the water jacket, it draws off heat.

AIRFLOW

COOLANT
RECOVERY
SYSTEM

THERMOSTAT

WATER PUMP

RADIATOR

**Cooling system
components**

3. The now-warm fluid flows back to the radiator via another hose, where it passes through a one-way, heat-sensitive door called a **thermostat**. Until the coolant reaches a predetermined temperature of about 180 to 205 degrees, the thermostat remains closed. This blocks the flow of coolant and forces it to recirculate around the combustion chambers. When the coolant finally reaches its normal operating temperature, the thermostat opens and the coolant flows back into the radiator. It then rushes down through the metal tubes where it is cooled—your car's equivalent of "sweating."

4. An electric fan or one powered by a belt which also serves the water pump pulls cool air from the outside through the radiator. The coolant is now ready to repeat its journey again and again.

5. Most cars today have a coolant recovery system. As coolant heats up, it expands. The overflow is stored in a translucent plastic container, the overflow reservoir, attached to the radiator. When the engine is turned off, the coolant contracts and is drawn back into the radiator from the overflow reservoir.

Coolant is a mixture of water and a chemical known as ethylene glycol, or antifreeze.

Just as sweat consists of more than water and includes other body chemicals, coolant is also a combination of water and a weird-looking chemical known as ethylene glycol, or **antifreeze**. When mixed with water, antifreeze keeps the water in your radiator from boiling in summer and freezing in winter. The liquid in your car's radiator should always—365 days a year—be coolant.

The right proportion of water to antifreeze for your car can be found—you guessed it—in your owner's manual. This proportion determines the coolant's range of temperature protection. Often it's a 50:50 ratio, which will protect an engine from freezing down to -34° F (2° C) and raise its boiling point from 226° to 263° F (113° to 151° C). Only if you live in Deadhorse, Alaska (or an exceedingly cold climate) should the proportion of antifreeze to water be as high as 70:30. This will protect an engine down to -84° F (-64° C). More than 70 percent antifreeze causes the protective qualities of coolant to disappear.

Without even removing the cap, you can see where the coolant is. If the coolant level is below the appropriate line, wait until the engine is cold, remove the cap on the reservoir, and add the mixture of antifreeze and water recommended in your owner's manual.

Making your car go the distance
The Cooling System

Assuming the correct level and proportion of coolant are maintained, and the water pump, thermostat, fan, and radiator cap are in working order, the correct temperature for the engine should be achieved. All it takes is a little TLC to make this driving dream a reality.

✔ Every other time you buy gas, or as often as each week during the summer, check to be sure there is plenty of coolant in the overflow reservoir.

✔ When topping off, use only antifreeze that states on the label "suitable for all engine types." This will ensure that it contains the special additives that protect all types of engine metals—aluminum as well as the more common cast iron.

✔ Be aware of changes in coolant consumption. If you are constantly replacing coolant, have the system inspected. Leaks don't always show up on your garage floor or in your driveway. *Some leaks only occur when the engine is under the higher pressures of highway driving.*

✔ Each year, get a professional maintenance check of the entire cooling system. The radiator, water pump, fan, thermostat, radiator cap, belts, hoses, clamps, and concentration of the antifreeze should be inspected. Any belt or hose that appears brittle, flaky, cracked, or mushy should be replaced at this time.

✔ Have the coolant system drained and flushed every year. All coolant loses its protective qualities eventually. When it does, water pumps and radiators deteriorate.

✔ The amount of coolant that is right for your car can be found in your owner's manual under "Liquid Capacity" or "Specifications."

Warning!
Never open the coolant reservoir or remove the radiator cap until you are absolutely certain the engine is cold. If the cap is removed while the engine is hot, the coolant could burst out of the radiator and the escaping steam could injure you.

When Something Goes Wrong with the Cooling System

Slow-moving traffic in summer can cause even the healthiest cooling system to overheat.

If your engine does overheat (your engine "temp" light goes on, or the temperature gauge moves into the "hot" zone), there are several things you can do to keep the repair bill somewhere below the national deficit.

1) Turn off the air conditioning; it makes the engine work 20 percent hotter; **2)** turn your car's heater to its hottest setting; **3)** turn the heater fan on. This will pull some of the heat away from the engine and into the passenger compartment. This might also be a good time to open the windows. Of course, now *you* will overheat, but remember, dry cleaning your suit is cheaper than rebuilding your engine. **4)** try to increase the distance between you and the car directly in front of you. Its tail pipe is sending out hot exhaust fumes that are making a bad problem worse.

If it's hot enough to stir-fry on the pavement, none of these strategies may help. If all else fails and your car is still overheating, it's time to turn your hazard lights on, get the car safely off the road, and turn the engine off and let it cool down. *Note:* No two emergency situations are alike. Your concern for your personal safety must guide your response.

If, after letting the system cool down, you check and find nothing apparently wrong, it is usually safe to drive the car, assuming the engine temperature or coolant indicator is normal. You may not even need to consult a technician.

Like a jogger who runs too many miles on a hot day and experiences heat exhaustion, your car may sometimes need to rest in the shade and get its fluid balance back. Listen to your car as you would to your body. Respond by giving each system a rest and replacing lost fluids before returning to a normal routine. Should the car continue to overheat, you probably have a more serious problem.

The Heating System

On some especially chilly winter days, it may feel like it takes forever to get yourself and your windshield defrosted. But, in fact, our modern automotive heating systems are models of efficiency and comfort, particularly in comparison with earlier heating methods. In the early days of motoring one had to be quite ingenious to overcome the sting of the elements. Pans of glowing briquettes were often placed on the floor in the passenger compartment; all kinds of wild motoring outfits were designed. Even as late as 1930, being comfortable inside a car in cold weather was considered a luxury.

If your car really is taking forever to warm up on a

The heating system. The different heater and defroster controls allow you to open and close the passageways leading inside the car, directing the heat to different places in the passenger compartment—up to the windshield for defrost, down to the passengers for comfort.

❖

cold morning, blame the cooling system, not the heater, for it is the coolant that actually warms you. The heater is actually a mini radiator and works in a similar way. When you turn on the heater/defroster button or lever in your car, heated coolant is diverted from its normal journey. Instead of flowing from the engine to the radiator, where most of its heat would have been released, the coolant is drawn by the water pump through a **heater control valve** (a one-way door) to a smaller radiator called the **heater core**, located directly in front of the passenger compartment. The hot coolant passes through the core and releases its heat. An electric fan then forces the warmth of the coolant into the passenger compartment through passageways called *ducts*.

A. C. Principles

(A) WHEN A LIQUID BECOMES A VAPOR (GAS), IT ABSORBS HEAT.

(B) WHEN A VAPOR BECOMES A LIQUID IT GIVES OFF HEAT.

(C) HEAT ALWAYS MOVES FROM A WARMER SPOT TO A COLDER SPOT

The Air Conditioning System

Air conditioning doesn't add cold; it removes heat. It accomplishes this by removing heat from one area and sending it to another through the use of a fluid called **refrigerant**. This process of absorbing and releasing heat is what cools the inside of our cars, our homes, and our refrigerators.

Although individual components may vary from car to car, the following basics apply to all air conditioning systems.

Refrigerant has a unique characteristic: it needs very

The air conditioning system

❖

little heat to bring it to a boil. In a car, refrigerant is circulated through an **evaporator**, or series of coils, located in front of the passenger compartment. An **expansion valve** (a one-way door) regulates the flow of refrigerant into the evaporator. As the refrigerant moves through the evaporator, it boils and absorbs heat from inside the car.

From the evaporator, the heated refrigerant moves to the **compressor**, a belt-driven pump. The compressor compresses the gas under extremely high pressure, dramatically raising the temperature of the refrigerant to more than 150° F (118° C).

From the compressor, the refrigerant goes to the **condenser**, which looks like a radiator and sits in front of the regular radiator. In the condenser, air cools the refrigerant and returns it to a liquid state. Just as it absorbed heat when it boiled, it now gives up its heat as it turns back into a liquid. As a high pressure liquid once again, the refrigerant flows to the **receiver dryer**, a filter that removes any moisture from the liquid. Air conditioning units hate moisture. A blower motor forces this cooled air into the car through vents.

Air conditioning doesn't add cold; it removes heat.

Known for many years as Freon, a chemical in the chlorofluorocarbons group, the refrigerant R-12 was the medium of choice for air conditioning systems. But research has now shown that it contributes to the depletion of the earth's ozone layer. In its place the refrigerant

Money-Saving Tip

To keep your air conditioning in good working order, run it for about five minutes once a week whenever the outside temperature is above 50° F (10° C). The many rubber components of this system dry out and crack if they are not lubricated by the oil that circulates with the refrigerant. This lubrication only takes place when the air conditioning is turned on.

R134a, a CFC-free refrigerant, has been substituted. From now on the refrigerant installed in all new vehicles will be R134a. *Note:* The two cannot be mixed. Using the wrong kind can damage the air conditioning unit.

Automatic Climate Control

The first attempts at air conditioning required bulky systems to provide the passenger compartment with cool air on a hot day. Today's systems are more streamlined.

Many cars are now equipped with a computer that controls passenger compartment temperatures. Electronic sensors detect temperatures within the passenger compartment and feed that information to the computer. The computer compares these temperatures against preset "ideal" temperatures. If the sensors register colder, the computer then directs an appropriate amount of warmed coolant to the passenger compartment. It also automatically opens and closes heating vents to allow just the right amount of warm air into the passenger compartment. When it's warm outside, the temperature control system also operates the air conditioning. Today, heating, air conditioning, and engine cooling are all tied together.

Many of today's cars are equipped with a computer that controls temperatures in the passenger compartment.

Frequently asked questions

Q Does it matter if an engine runs cold?

A You bet it does—and the consequences can be serious. Engines that do not reach their "ideal" temperatures retain moisture and do not burn off the by-products of combustion—carbon deposits. These deposits build up inside engines causing excess stress, heat, and premature engine wear. There are a number of reasons why an engine will run cold. Two of the most common causes are a faulty thermostat that never closes (and so the coolant never warms adequately) and a low coolant level. Poor fuel economy usually accompanies a cold engine.

Making your car go the distance
Temperature Control Systems

✓ To cool properly, the air conditioning system must have the correct amount of refrigerant. This amount is specific to your car and needs to be recharged periodically. Most modern shops recharge by capturing the old refrigerant and recycling it.

✓ Have all air conditioning components inspected according to the service schedule in your owner's manual.

✓ Conversions to R134a are currently being developed by the manufacturers and differ widely from car to car. Check with your dealership to determine if there is any warranty coverage.

Warning!

Fixing the air conditioning system is a job for a properly equipped professional. The refrigerant boils at a very low temperature and can easily burn the skin. In contact with a flame or other heat source, it can change into a poisonous gas. And adding too much freon can result in an explosion.

Troubleshooting the Cooling System

Symptoms	Low coolant, incorrect mixture	Slipping belt	Inoperative electric cooling fan*	Faulty radiator cap	Worn or broken water pump	Clogged radiator pump hose or coolant passages	Leaking internally or externally**	Sending unit sensor incorrect timing	Faulty gauge warning light	Thermostat
Engine overheats	●	●	●	●	●	●	●	●	●	●
Engine runs too cold								●	●	
Loss of coolant				●	●		●			

*Fan fuse, wiring, ground, switch, relay, clutch, motor.
**Radiator, hose, coolant recovery tank, water pump, leaky head gasket, blown head gasket, leaking core plugs, internal cracks in engine.

Troubleshooting the Heating and AC Systems

Symptoms	Low or high refrigerant charge	Clogged radiator, heater, core, or kinked hose	Slipping belt	Blower motor, fuse, switch, wiring or ground	Heater control valve	Temperature or vent lever binding or broken	A/C clutch, fuse, switch, wiring, ground	Restrictions in condensor	Air lock in system	Clogged A/C drain	Computer-related**
No heat, no defrost*	●	●		●	●	●			●		●
Insufficient heat	●	●		●	●	●			●		●
Heater blows hot and cold									●		
No air conditioning	●			●		●					
Insufficient air conditioning	●		●	●	●	●	●	●		●	
Mildew odor										●	

*If you are experiencing defroster difficulty in your imported vehicle:
1. Move the air intake lever or button to "fresh"
2. Turn the blower on high setting
3. Set the temp control to "hot"
4. Switch the air conditioner to "on." See if the defroster works now

**On vehicles with electronic climate control, a technician will need to follow the manufacturer's service manual for diagnosing problems.

10
The Drive Train

Whether you drive a rear-wheel, front-
wheel, four-wheel, or all-wheel drive vehicle, the transmissions that transmit power from
the engine to the wheels are complex, and
their repairs can be expensive. Learning about
them will help you to avoid a shiftless transmission. With the right preventive maintenance you
can expect smaller and fewer repair bills. ❖

REAR WHEEL DRIVE

FRONT WHEEL
DRIVE

FOUR WHEEL
DRIVE

**In a rear-wheel drive car, only the rear wheels receive
power. In a front-wheel drive car, only the front
wheels receive power. In four-wheel and all-wheel
drive cars, however, all four wheels receive power.**

❖

The drive train consists of those components that pass
along or transmit power from the engine to the wheels.
In most cars only two wheels receive power. While drive

Gears are round metal wheels with teeth.

❖

trains vary in their design, there are a number of components that are common to all. These include *transmissions* and the metal linkage that connects the transmission to the wheels.

Let's return to the analogy of the bicyclist for a moment. Remember that it was through the bicycle chain that the energy produced by the pumping action of the bicyclist's legs was passed along to the bicycle wheels? Look more closely at that bicycle chain and you will see a series of round metal toothed wheels that we call gears. Peel back the skin of most transmissions and you will also find a series of gears.

Gears are necessary because cars and bicyclists are subject to **inertia**, the force that places resistance on a car's forward motion from a dead stop. However, once the car is moving, its heavy weight, which had made it so difficult to move initially, is now the factor that keeps it moving. **Momentum** has taken over.

To compensate for these natural forces, cars need slow, powerful turns from their wheels to get started and when traveling up hills. But they need speedy turns from their wheels when they're traveling at normal highway speeds. To meet the changing needs of the car, the energy produced by the engine has to be transmitted differently to the car's wheels—sometimes powerfully, sometimes speedily, sometimes not at all. The gears inside the trans-

"GEARS WORK on the PRINCIPLE THAT THE FASTER THE ENGINE TURNS IN RELATION TO THE WHEELS THE MORE POWER (TORQUE) IS PRODUCED"

mission make it possible to meet those different needs. The transmission is the "link" between the engine and the wheels.

How Gears Work

Gears are always found in sets. Assuming that their teeth are meshed together, when one gear turns the other gear also turns. To see how gears really work, let's start with first gear. Let's assume the big gear with 40 teeth is attached to the wheels, and the small gear with ten teeth is attached to the engine. How many times will the small gear go around in the time it takes the large gear to go around once? If you answered "four," you rocket to the head of the class. The effort of four speedy turns of the engine is transferred into one powerful turn of the wheel. This relationship is expressed as a **gear ratio**. The gear ratio for this set of gears is 4:1. This gear ratio works well for a car that is starting out from a dead stop because it provides the greatest amount of torque or twisting power from the engine to the wheels. The

1ST GEAR

2ND GEAR

3RD GEAR

4TH GEAR

5TH GEAR

Gears are always found in sets. Here are gears one through five.

"lower" the gear, the more power and less speed is delivered to the wheels.

As the car continues to move forward, having broken with the force of inertia, it needs less power and more speed. In second gear, the gear attached to the wheels may have 30 teeth and the gear attached to the engine may have ten teeth. Three speedy turns of the input shaft are transferred into one slower turn of the output shaft

Frequently asked questions

Q What is fifth gear, or an **overdrive** gear?

A In a **manual** (standard) **transmission**, a fifth gear (or an overdrive gear in an automatic transmission) takes advantage of the car's momentum. When being driven at highway speeds, a car needs speed, not power. It requires fewer crankshaft turns from the engine. Since the engine doesn't work as hard, it doesn't use as much gas. Consequently, you save money by using fifth gear, or overdrive, at highway speeds.

With a manual transmission, you select the gear appropriate for the driving conditions.

(gear ratio 3:1). Second gear is still a powerful gear but not as powerful as first. Eventually, when the car reaches highway speeds, the force of momentum has taken over. Consequently, in fourth (depending on the gear box), both gears are turning at the same speed (gear ratio 3:3). All cars have at least three gears, plus reverse, and many have four, five, or even six.

Manual Transmissions

There are two types of transmissions: manual (standard) and automatic. With a manual or standard transmission,

SHIFTING FORK

SYNCHRONIZER COLLAR

POWER IMPUT FROM ENGINE

POWER OUTPUT TO WHEELS

1ST REVERSE 2ND 3RD 4TH

A manual transmission

❖

you select the gear appropriate for the driving conditions by moving a gear shift or lever. With an automatic transmission the gears are selected for you.

The earliest gears actually moved into and out of each other, sometimes meshing smoothly, sometimes not. When two gears meshed together their separate movements had to be coordinated or—*crunch, crunch*—the gear teeth bumped into each other. The result was missing teeth and frequent gear replacement. Then came synchronizers.

Synchronizers are rings with teeth that point out ("dogs") and collars with teeth that point in. It is the synchronizers that actually move, not the gears. The gear ratios are already locked together. This makes for smooth shifting, few crunches, and very little wear on the gears themselves. Thus, the gears rarely wear out; the synchronizers do instead. Such a deal.

The Clutch

If your car has a manual transmission, it also has a **clutch**. Located between the engine and the transmission, the clutch makes it possible for the engine to

COLLAR FREEWHEELING GEAR

CONE DOGS

DOGS

SPLINES

SYNCHRONIZER →

Synchronizers are rings with teeth that point out and collars with teeth that point in. It is the synchronizers that actually move, not the gears.

The clutch connects and disconnects the engine from the wheels.

CRANKSHAFT

GEAR SHIFT LEVER

TO ENGINE

TO DRIVESHAFT

CLUTCH

TRANSMISSION GEARS

change gears. The clutch connects and disconnects the engine from the rest of the drive train. By disconnecting the transmission from the engine, the clutch allows the engine to continue to run without transmitting its power to the wheels.

How the Clutch Works

Clutch designs vary, but most have the same basic components—the flywheel, several steel plates or discs that slide along a shaft, a round metal doughnut called a **throw-out bearing**, and a metal arm called a **release fork**. As you know from chapter 4, the flywheel is attached to the crankshaft (the bar that holds onto the pistons). Next in line is a plate called the **clutch disc**, which is covered with a tough layer of friction material,

When the clutch pedal is released, the engine and wheels are connected. When the clutch pedal is depressed, the engine is disconnected from the wheels.

CLUTCH DISC

THROW-OUT BEARING

CLUTCH DISENGAGED (PEDAL DEPRESSED)

FLYWHEEL   PRESSURE PLATE

CLUTCH DISC

THROW-OUT BEARING

CLUTCH ENGAGED (PEDAL RELEASED)

FLYWHEEL CONNECTED TO ENGINE

FLYWHEEL   PRESSURE PLATE

Gasoline-powered automobiles were first developed in the late 19th century. The early cars represented dramatic advancements in engineering, but they were relatively simple machines compared to the cars of today. The average mechanically-inclined individual could perform even major repairs to cars that were manufactured through the 1960s. Today's vehicles, however, are much more complex.

▲ The single-front-wheel design of this 1903 Duryea was mechanically simple. But the advantages of dual front wheels—stability and a smooth ride—soon pushed the single-wheel approach aside.

▲ Women have taken responsibility for maintaining their own autos since cars first hit the roads. Although few drivers do their own repairs today, understanding the basics of how a car works remains important.

▼ Cars have always been multipurpose vehicles—even the earliest owners seemed to find a use for all the "storage space" cars offered.

▲ Cars are vehicles of liberation. Proper maintenance of your car can keep it on the road for a long time.

▲ Introduced in 1908, Henry Ford's Model T was the first dependable car that an average person (or a local fire department) could afford. The Model T was the first car to be produced entirely on an assembly line, and it became the most popular car in the world, manufactured in the U.S. and in more than 20 plants in other countries.

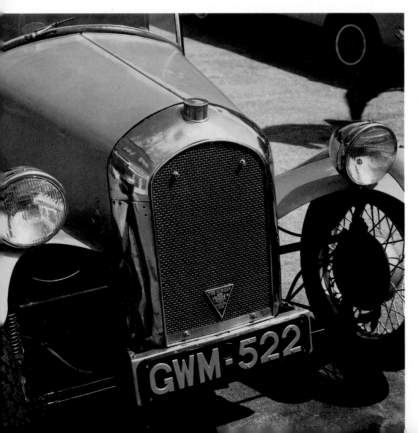

◄

The Morgan is still being manufactured in a small factory in Middlesex, England, where craftsmen shape its frame from wood and hand-assemble every piece of the vehicle. Pictured is a 1933 model.

GWM·522

▲ This 1936 Mercedes-Benz was produced in an era when design was as important as performance in a luxury automobile. An elongated hood and prominent, sweeping fenders were thought to be the height of sophistication.

▼ Cars like this one conjure images of gangsters and G-men with tommy guns. This 1936 Mercedes-Benz limousine was built to be bullet-proof. They say mechanics always charged reasonable rates and provided courteous service to owners of these cars.

▲ Design fads have produced some extraordinary looking cars over the years. This magnificent 1939 Talbot Lago aerodynamic coupe exemplifies the importance of design in the luxury car market.

▼ Classically designed cars such as this 1937 Chevy are sometimes used as vehicles of modern expression. This car has been customized into a "low-rider" look.

▲ In this 1938 Peugeot Eclipse, French designers demonstrated how the practical needs of exterior lights and an air intake can be combined to make a design statement.

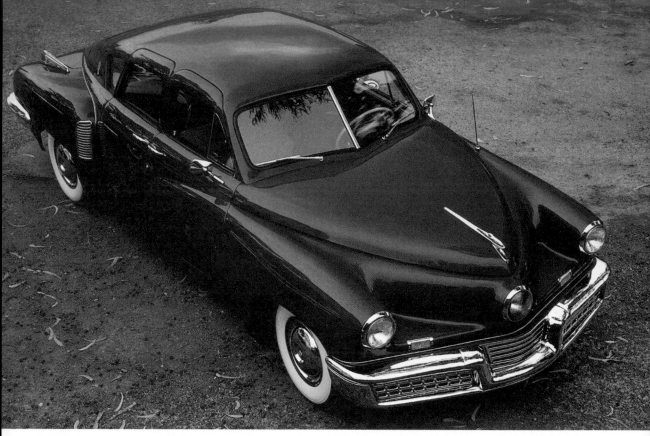

▲ Preston Tucker followed his dream and in 1948 began manufacturing and marketing his own automobile, the Tucker Torpedo. He was unable to compete with the major car companies and never produced large quantites of the Torpedo. Yet thanks to his entrepreneurial spirit, Tucker—and his car—remain American legends.

▼ In the 1940s and 1950s, wood was often used for exterior ornamentation, as seen on this 1948 Town & Country which boasts wood side panels. In those days car care included yearly sanding and revarnishing.

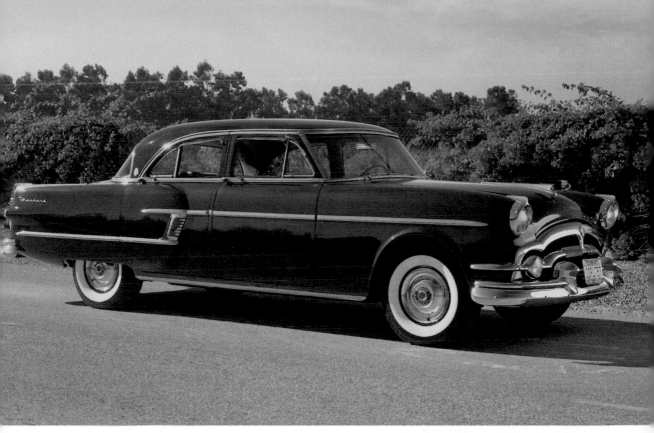

▲ The Packard was an expensive U.S. luxury car built to compete with the Cadillac and the Pierce-Arrow, as well as with foreign imports such as the Rolls-Royce, Talbot, and Bugatti.

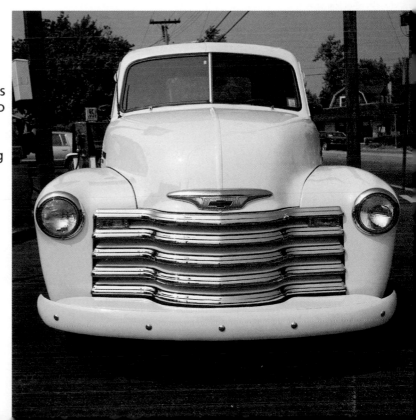

➤

The pick-up truck represents a direct link to our pre-auto past: the days when horse-drawn wagons with open rear beds carried everything from groceries and fence posts to chicken feed, kids, and dogs.

▲ European automakers were the leaders in design for decades. Here the designers of the expensive, luxurious, and fast Talbot Lago have fashioned front-end lighting into a work of art.

▲ For several decades the hood ornament was an important feature of a car's design. Ornaments were simple to maintain and beautiful to behold. This one sat atop the 1955 Chevy Bel-Air.

▼ Few American-made cars captured the spirit of the times better than the early Ford Thunderbirds. Like this 1955 model, they had peppy but simple engines that many owners could tune and repair themselves.

▲ This German-made 1956 Porsche is a living legend. Loved by ordinary drivers as well as by racing enthusiasts, these high-performance cars have complex precision systems that can be difficult to keep in tune and expensive to repair.

▼ The classic Chevrolet Bel-Air was the car of choice for millions of Americans. This 1957 model appeared before designers took the art of tail fins to its extreme.

▲ Car manufacturers have made their share of mistakes, and none is more legendary than Ford's introduction of the Edsel in 1957. Designed and priced for a class of consumers that never showed up, they were discontinued in 1959.

▼ For decades the Chevrolet Impala was loved for its sleek design, dependability, roomy interior, and powerful V-8 engine. This 1959 convertible shows the era's delight with tail fins and other imaginative design features.

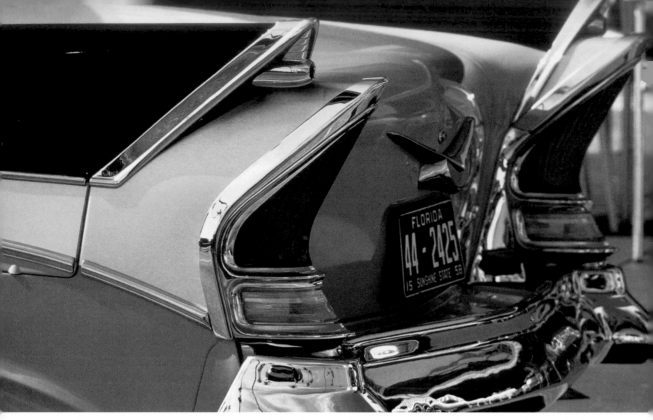

▲ When chrome was king, the Cadillac had to have more of it than any other vehicle on the road. As this model shows, elaborate designs were often accompanied by two—and occasionally three—different paint colors.

▼ For decades the word "Cadillac" was synonymous in America with "biggest," "best," and "most expensive." This 1959 model was produced at the height of America's fascination with tail fins. At that time, even Cadillac's *fins* had fins.

Few cars have had as great an impact on American culture as the Volkswagen Beetle. It was at once bizarre-looking (by the standards of the 1960s), surprisingly fuel efficient, peppy, and fun to drive. The company that publishes this book was founded in 1969 when John Muir self-published the now-classic *How to Keep Your Volkswagen Alive: A Manual of Step-by-Step Procedures for the Compleat Idiot.*

➤

By 1964, Ford's Thunderbird had grown from a small sports car to a large luxury model. Ford introduced the now-classic Mustang to satisfy the many middle-class Americans who still dreamed of owning a sports car.

▲ This side-view of the high-performance Auto-Zara prototype reveals the ever-increasing complexity of today's automobiles.

◄

The futuristic, solar-powered "Mana La" is perhaps a model of alternative-powered cars to come.

Since the 1960s, automobiles have become increasingly complex. Expensive tools and electronic diagnostic equipment are now needed to properly tune and repair most cars. As automotive technology and engineering continue to evolve, car owners need to keep up with the basics to be able to properly maintain their vehicles and speak intelligently with their mechanics.

and finally there is the **pressure plate**. A throw-out bearing and a release fork secure the components to the shaft.

When the clutch pedal is released, the pressure plate squeezes the clutch disc against the flywheel. Consequently, the clutch begins to turn at the same rate as the

Money-Saving Tip

Depending on the gear selected, the clutch disc will go from rest (zero turns) or no revolutions per minute (rpms) to as many as 5,000 rpms or more in a fraction of a second! Just before the connection with the flywheel is complete, the disc experiences a slipping motion that results in friction. Friction causes heat and heat causes wear.

Do not use your clutch pedal for a foot rest. It makes a very bad one. "Riding the clutch" can burn out a clutch in a short period of time. Keep your foot off the clutch pedal when not in use; engage it and disengage it quickly.

flywheel. The engine is now connected to the transmission and the wheels.

When the clutch pedal is depressed, the engine is disconnected from the wheels. Consequently, the clutch disc, which had been squeezed against the flywheel, separates from it. The transmission is now in neutral. Power will not flow to the wheels until the clutch pedal is released again.

The clutch disc

Automatic Transmissions

In an automatic transmission, the gears are shifted automatically. Instead of a clutch, an automatic transmission has a **torque converter**.

The torque converter is a housing filled with two fans

An automatic transmission

❖

With an automatic transmission, the gears are selected for you.

and a lightweight oil called **transmission fluid**. One fan is called an **impeller** and is attached to the engine. The other fan is called a **turbine** and is attached to the transmission. As the engine's crankshaft rotates, the impeller turns. If the impeller is turning fast enough, the other fan turns. The more speed the engine develops, the faster the fans spin.

The fans' motion pressurizes the fluid within tiny passageways in the **valve control body**. Here the fluid moves a series of metal components called bands (collars) and clutches which change the gears. All the driver has to do is to step on the gas.

How the torque converter works: when the plugged-in fan is turned on, it blows air into the second fan, causing it to turn. This is analogous to the action of the impeller on the turbine.

Planetary gears

❖

Planetary Gears

The gears within an automatic transmission are called **planetary gears**. They may not look like the ones within a manual transmission, but the principle is the same: sets of gears (two, three, four, or more, depending on the gearbox, plus reverse) provide the necessary speed or power appropriate for different driving conditions.

In an automatic transmission, the gears move around each other in a circle. Each gear set consists of an outer **ring gear** within which sits a central **sun gear** flanked by smaller planet gears. Just as you might expect, these smaller planet gears move around the sun gear. Gears are selected by locking and releasing specific gear sets.

Electronically Controlled Transmissions

Many of today's transmissions are computer controlled and remarkably efficient. These "smart" transmissions use a computer to track input from several different sources, including the pressure on the accelerator pedal, and crunch the data as many as 30 times per second. The computer can recognize a quick accelerator movement and downshift at just the right time—as efficiently as most drivers could do manually. In addition, many of the cost benefits that were traditionally associated with the fuel economy of manual transmissions are quickly disappearing as electronic transmissions use the speed of computers to do our shifting for us.

Money-Saving Tip

Never rock your car back and forth in a snow bank more than a few times. It overheats the transmission.

Final Drive for the Rear-Wheel Drive Car

Final drive includes the components that finish or finalize the transmission of power from the engine to the wheels. **Rear-wheel drive** vehicles transmit power only to the rear wheels. Front-wheel drive vehicles transmit power only to the front wheels. This method saves space and provides superior traction on slippery surfaces. Four-wheel and all-wheel drive vehicles can transmit power of all four wheels, providing awesome grip.

In a rear-wheel drive vehicle, power is transferred from the transmission to the car's rear wheels via a long turning bar or shaft, called a **driveshaft**. The driveshaft is

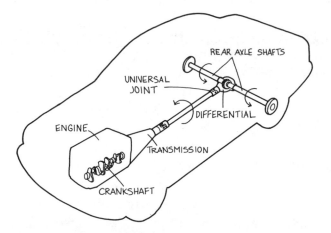

In a rear-wheel drive car, power is transferred to the rear wheels via a long turning bar called the driveshaft.

The differential allows the outside wheels to travel farther and faster than the inside wheels.

❖

attached to the **differential**. This special set of gears does two things: (1) It takes the power of the engine and transmission and turns it at a right angle to the rear axles that connect the rear wheels. (2) The differential allows the wheels to travel at different speeds when cornering. This is necessary because the outer wheels follow a larger arc than the inner wheels when the vehicle turns.

Final Drive for the Front-Wheel Drive Car

In a **front-wheel drive** car, the differential is moved forward and combined with the transmission into one unit

In a front-wheel drive car, the differential is moved forward and combined with the transmission into one unit called the transaxle.

called the **transaxle**. Power follows a more indirect path before it reaches the shorter axles (stub axles) that are connected to the front wheels.

Four-Wheel Drive

In recent years the technology that transfers power to all four wheels has led to a whole generation of **four-wheel drive** passenger cars and light trucks from which to choose. Not only are there many manufacturers designing four-wheel drive vehicles, but they are doing it in several different ways.

Traditional four-wheel drive transfers power to the rear wheels through a differential. It can also transfer power to all four wheels through a **transfer case**. This special third set of gears, which is typically engaged through a shift lever, can lock the front and rear axles together. When power is transferred to all four wheels, traction is increased.

Part-time four-wheel drive vehicles have an interior shift lever to make locking and unlocking the two axles easy and convenient. To make them even more convenient, a number of systems have been developed which allow the driver to shift into four-wheel drive while the vehicle is moving.

Four-wheel drive

All-wheel drive

❖

All-wheel drive

All-wheel drive systems use electronics to transfer power to where it is most needed. The result is awesome grip and the advantages of four-wheel drive, without the added fuel consumption.

Among the variations of all-wheel drive is a system that connects the front and rear axles by means of metal plates attached to each, which are then bathed in a special coupling fluid. Under normal driving conditions, the plates are not connected. Power flows to one axle only as it would in any front- or rear-wheel drive car. But if one wheel loses traction and starts spinning, the temperature of the coupling fluid changes and it thickens. The thickened fluid locks the two metal plates and also locks the two axles together. With both axles "live," all four wheels are now receiving power. Unless you're buried up to your eyeballs in mud or snow, the car should be able to get enough traction to move.

All-wheel drive systems transfer power to where it is most needed, resulting in superior traction without added fuel consumption.

When the car returns to dry pavement, the good traction sends a signal to the fluid, the temperature of which changes back to normal, and the plates relax and disconnect. Power flows once again to one axle only.

U-joints and CV Joints

Universal joints, or "U-joints," are metal joints designed like human wrists. In a rear-wheel or four-wheel drive

UNIVERSAL
JOINT

HUMAN
JOINT

U-joints are metal joints designed like human joints .

❖

vehicle, these coupling mechanisms facilitate movement
between the transmission and the driveshaft, and the
driveshaft and the differential. To see how U-joints work,
keep your arm still and wave your hand up and down.
The wrist motion is a simple flex, isn't it? Your hand is
ideally designed with ligaments and muscles to help you
perform this flexing motion many, many times without
you having to do anything to maintain it. But a U-joint,
because it's metal, needs a special lubricant for protection.
A thick dark grease coats the joint to prevent friction from
causing premature wear. U-joints are now pre-lubed and
sealed at the factory (as are most other couplers).

The front-wheel drive version of a U-joint is a **CV**
(constant velocity) **joint**. CV joints are designed like
human elbows. On front-wheel drive cars, the short or
"stub" axles must be able to transfer the up-and-down
motion of the road as well as the side-to-side motion of
the steering. Consequently, a more complicated connector is required. CV joints are the answer. To see how a
CV joint works, hold your right elbow in your left palm
and rotate it. Now compare that motion to the simple
flexing motion of your wrist. The more complex the
motion, the more complex the mechanism. The expensive-

CV joints are designed like human elbows.

❖

to-replace ball bearings inside the CV joints are protected with lubricating grease and sealed with rubber covers called "boots."

Money-Saving Tip

A CV joint often warns us of problems by making a clicking sound that can be heard coming from the front wheels, typically when the car is turning a corner. If you hear this warning sound, have the CV joints inspected by a professional for damage as soon as possible. If a slight tear in the boot is discovered early enough, you may only have to replace it, not the joint. Replacing the boot is much less expensive than replacing a failed joint.

Making your car go the distance
The Drive Train

If transmissions sound complex, they are. If they sound like they could be expensive to fix, they can be. *But* they don't have to be. Here are a few ways to avoid transmission problems.

✓ Limit the weight you carry on long trips even if it means shipping some things—particularly if you are driving into the mountains. Carrying a heavy load,

Overloading and overtowing can cause transmission damage.

❖

especially uphill, can cause a transmission to overheat, and overheating is a major cause of transmission damage.

Don't tear out of the driveway as soon as you start your engine. Give your car a full minute to warm up before you put it in gear.

✓ Much transmission damage occurs in the morning before the transmission fluid has reached the hundreds of delicate metal parts. Jumping in your car and throwing it in reverse is one sure way to harm a transmission. Give the car a full minute to warm up before you put it in gear.

✓ When you know the car will have a difficult task, like lugging a heavy load uphill, choose a lower gear.

Read your owner's manual for an explanation of how to use these gears. Your transmission will appreciate it.

✔ If you are doing a lot of severe driving (towing a trailer, for example), consider having your car equipped with a extra transmission cooler. (Check your owner's manual for any special requirements.)

✔ Don't shift into park or reverse until the vehicle has come to a complete stop.

✔ Have the transmission and clutch (if appropriate) adjusted to manufacturer's specifications. Doing so reduces wear, improves performance, and helps you to avoid expensive repairs.

✔ Have your CV boots checked for damage whenever the car is up on a lift. It's a simple visual check that only takes a minute but can save you hundreds of dollars.

The proper procedure for checking automatic transmission fluid varies from car to car. Your owner's manual tells you how. Here is one method.

❖

✔ Check the automatic transmission fluid level or have it checked once a month. In addition to making your transmission shift correctly, transmission fluid protects the delicate internal parts from wear.

✓ Have the transmission fluid, final-drive fluids, and the transmission filter changed as often as your owner's manual recommends.

✓ Manual transmission fluid, final-drive fluid, and transfer case fluids should be checked by a professional every six months or as often as your owner's manual recommends. All are easily checked while the car is on a lift.

Troubleshooting the Drive Train

Possible causes

Symptoms	Low, incorrect or contaminated fluid, kinked lines	Dirty transmission filter	AT-linkage bands out of adjustment	Clutch out of adjustment	External fluid leaks, AT* and MT	Faulty u-joint or cv joint	Worn/broken transmission mount	Internal damage to transmission	Unbalanced/worn driveshaft/axle shafts	High idle speed	Computer-related, * AT	Clutch worn out, MT
AT–Delayed shifts	●	●	●		●						●	
AT–Rough shifts	●	●	●					●			●	
AT–No drive, slipping	●							●			●	
Loss of transmission fluid					●							
Transmission fluid overheats	●							●		●		
MT–Hard shifting	●			●								●
MT–Grinding noise	●			●								
MT–Slipping clutch				●	●							●
Thump/clunk in reverse						●	●	●	●			
Clicking while turning						●						
Vibration high speeds						●			●			
Humming sound from transmission	●							●				

AT–Automatic
MT–Manual or standard
*Seals, gaskets, lines

11
Steering and Suspension

This chapter describes how suspension and steering work together to help your vehicle hold the road. The more responsive your vehicle is, the safer it is. Repair done to suspension and steering systems, often referred to as "front end" work, is one area in which consumers are at higher than normal risk of being overcharged and sold unnecessary work. In this chapter, you will learn how to avoid that fate. ❖

The steering and suspension systems are analogous to the wrists, elbows, and knees of the human body.

The steering system

❖

Steering and suspension are kindred spirits. **Steering** is about controlling the right, left, and straight directional movements of your car; **suspension** is about controlling its up-and-down movement as it travels over the uneven road surface. These two systems not only share some of the same components, they each contribute to the other's performance. They also affect your safety since they heavily influence a car's "handling."

The suspension system

❖

How Steering Systems Work

Steering mechanisms are a combination of rods, levers, and gears that help you to maneuver your 2,000-pound-plus hunk of metal and rubber. There are two types of steering systems available for most cars: **parallelogram** or **rack and pinion**.

The Parallelogram Steering System

In the parallelogram steering system, the steering wheel is attached to a **steering shaft** that sits inside the **steering column**. As the steering wheel is turned, the rotational movement is transferred down the shaft to a **steering**

Steering and suspension influence a car's "handling."

The parallelogram steering system

gearbox. In combination with a series of connecting rods and levers, steering gears convert the circular motion of the steering column into the side-to-side motion of the wheels. Gears also take the force you exert on the steering wheel and magnify it many, many times, thus making the Herculean task of maneuvering your 2,000-pound-plus car easy—almost.

Rack and Pinion Steering

"Rack and pinion" may sound like a method of medieval torture, but it's really the popular, compact, and lightweight steering mechanism found in most modern cars. Rack and pinion steering eliminates the traditional steering gearbox and replaces it with a simpler set of gears: a toothed wheel called a **pinion gear** is attached to the end of the steering shaft, where it meets a long bar, or rack, that also has teeth. Rods and levers called **tie rods** and **steering arms** attach the rack to the wheels.

Rack and pinion steering eliminates the traditional steering gearbox and replaces it with a simpler set of gears.

❖

Power Steering

In the early days, cars ran on very narrow tires and were extremely responsive to the least guidance from the

Money-Saving Tip

Rack and pinion systems are bathed in lubricant coverings called "boots" Rubber seals keep the lubricant in and the dirt out. Like most rubber, the seals shrink and crack with age, especially in cold

Boots and seals in the rack and pinion system can shrink and crack with age.

weather. If you notice the steering wheel is hard to turn on cold mornings, have the steering inspected. A bit of special lubricant applied by a professional and specifically made for revitalizing seals may help. If the steering rack is faulty, you may even be entitled to special goodwill compensation from your manufacturer if this is a well-known problem.

steering wheel. Driving these cars may have been easy on the driver's arms but not so on their legs, for the driver and passengers often walked home after the car skittered off the road. To be up close and personal with ditches was not a desired condition, but it was a frequent one.

With the introduction and acceptance of wider tires, vehicles stayed on the road better, but they were more difficult to park in small spaces. Parking a car weighing more than 2,000 pounds became a chore fit only for weightlifters.

Power steering adds the turning power of the engine to the turning power of the steering gears. This assistance comes from a belt-driven power steering pump. This pump pressurizes the power steering fluid, which is held in a reservoir. The fluid pressure increases turning power. Consequently, less manual pressure is needed to turn the steering wheel.

Power steering uses a pump driven by a belt to pressurize fluid. If the belts break, you can still steer, but you will need to use more muscle.

If the belt for the pump breaks or the fluid in the reservoir is too low, the power assist may be lost. You will still be able to steer, but you'll have to really crank on that steering wheel to get it to turn.

Variable Ratio Power Steering (Computer Assisted)

One side effect of power assist is a diminished sense of connection to the road. To compensate, some manufacturers now electronically reduce the power assist to the steering when you're traveling at highway speeds, where the extra boost is not needed, and reinstate it when you're traveling at slower speeds. This **variable ratio power** steering makes it easy to park without losing that good "road feel" when driving.

Suspension

The suspension system supports the body and chassis and attaches them to the wheels. Suspension is also the system that gives us a nice comfortable ride. Were it not for your car's suspension, every time you went over a bump, the car would bounce, and bounce, and bounce.

Suspension helps to control vehicle ride.

Ad nauseam. But the suspension is even more important to your safety than to your comfort. The suspension components help to keep the tires in constant contact with the road.

For many years automobiles were designed "body-on-frame"—a metal body that included the passenger compartment, hood, trunk, and fenders was attached to a steel frame that included the power train, steering, and suspension. Most vehicles today use a frameless "unibody" design; both frame and body are made of metal panels that are welded together. These changes have made cars far more comfortable and airtight. They have also made simple suspension components not so simple.

Most vehicles today use a frameless "unibody" design, which means that both frame and body are made of panels that are welded together.

Comfort and Control

The suspension's job is to provide passengers with the most comfortable ride and drivers with the best possible road handling. Suspension designs vary widely, but they include similar components: **springs**, **shock absorbers**, **struts**, and metal arms. These parts, often assisted by a computer, are combined in various sizes and shapes in both the front and the rear of the car.

The difference between the front and rear suspension components is largely determined by their task. Since the rear wheels don't steer, they have fewer angles to contend with. But the amount of weight that has to be distributed properly by the rear suspension varies more than it does for the front. And in rear-wheel drive cars, the rear also has to transfer the turning power of the engine.

Before the days of rubber tires, every bump from every rock and uneven bit of roadway was transferred directly through the wheels to the seats. With the development of air-filled rubber tires, passengers were isolated from rough road surfaces. Air-filled tires, however, generated a lot of unwanted "bounce for the ounce." To isolate passengers from this movement, different types of springs were developed.

Types of Front and Rear Suspensions

Each wheel is attached to the frame of the car by metal arms called **control arms**. The name of each is determined by its shape and its location (upper or lower). For example, A-arms are made in the triangular shape of the letter A. A wishbone is made in the shape of—surprise, surprise—a wishbone. A control arm may be upper, lower, or trailing (that is, it may trail behind the frame or cross member).

Springs compress to absorb the impact of wheels hitting a bump. When the car passes to level ground,

| Torsion bar | Leaf spring | Coil springs Double wishbone | Coil springs Trailing arm |

they extend to release this motion. They act like the body's knees. Springs are attached to the car by combining them with arms and wishbones to give a smooth ride and to help the vehicle hold the road properly. The three main types of springs are coil springs, leaf springs, and torsion bars.

Coil springs, the most common ones in use today on passenger cars, look like oversized metal Slinkies as they compress and extend again and again (in response to the irregularities in the road surface), before returning to their original shape. **Leaf springs** absorb the motion of the wheels as the uneven strips of metal of which they're made flatten and unflatten. They are still found on many four-wheel drive vehicles and in the rear of light trucks and some domestic passenger cars. **Torsion bars** absorb the road motion by means of a bar that twists and turns as the motion is received.

Shock Absorbers

Any type of spring would keep compressing and extending until we were begging for Dramamine if it weren't for shock absorbers, which work like a door closure, the kind with the metal tube that allows the door to open freely and close slowly. By absorbing some of the motion, the fluid in the door closure controls the speed at which the door returns to its original position. In a similar way, the shock absorber controls the up-and-down movement of the spring.

SHOCK ABSORBER

Like a door closure, the shock absorber absorbs the motion of the springs.

Like the door closure, the shock absorber is a sealed system filled with fluid; it contains two tubes that share a common center and a piston. The top of the shock absorber tube is attached to the frame of the car; the bottom is attached to a suspension arm. As the car moves up and down, the fluid is pushed through tiny openings, allowing the piston to move up and down faster or slower, depending on the size of the openings. This reduces the amount of up-and-down motion that is transferred to the passenger compartment (the smoothness or bumpiness of the ride).

Specialized Shock Absorbers

A variety of shock absorbers have been developed in recent years for the purpose of giving passengers the most comfortable ride, with the greatest control, and under a variety of different load conditions. Here are the main types.

MacPherson struts are one of a variety of specialized shock absorbers available on modern vehicles. They are particularly popular because they combine some of the traditional suspension components and eliminate others to make a smaller, lighter, more compact unit. They are found in almost all front-wheel drive vehicles and in the front of many rear-wheel drive vehicles as well.

MacPherson struts combine the spring and shock absorber into one unit. This design results in greater stability and improved road handling, which is why MacPherson struts are believed to be superior to many other suspensions in which the shock and the spring are separate.

PISTON ROD

PISTON

The shock absorber contains two tubes that share a common center and a piston.

Frequently asked questions

Q How often should shock absorbers be replaced?

A Check your owner's manual for the manufacturer's recommendations, but keep in mind that it's a good idea to have your original shock absorbers and struts checked after 25,000 miles (40,500 kilometers), then every 15,000 miles (24,300 kilometers). Worn shocks or struts can increase wear and tear of your car's tires, suspension, and steering components.

Heavy-duty Shock Absorbers

A MacPherson strut combines the spring and shock absorber into one unit.

Heavy-duty shocks are regular shock absorbers but larger in size and with more fluid. The more fluid, the more motion the shock absorber can absorb. A heavy-duty shock absorber can handle greater loads and keep the wheels planted firmly on the ground, but the ride is harsher. These replacement shock absorbers are worth considering if your car frequently tows heavy loads.

Gas-powered Shock Absorbers

After a heavy workout, any shock absorber is prone to "fading." Fading occurs when a shock absorber works too hard, for example, riding on rough, unpaved roads. In response to this excessive demand, one tube moves rapidly and continuously inside the other, causing air bubbles to form inside the tubes. The shock absorber becomes temporarily less efficient and the quality of the ride is consequently diminished. Endless bouncing takes place even if the shocks are new. **Gas-powered shock absorbers** were developed as one response to this problem.

Gas-powered shock absorbers, which are becoming standard on many newer model cars, use a nitrogen charge to pressurize the fluid in the piston. Under pressure, air bubbles can't form. The shock absorbers maintain a steady performance, providing a smooth ride

After a heavy workout, any shock absorber is prone to "fading," becoming temporarily less efficient.

regardless of the difficulty or the unfriendliness of the terrain.

Variable Load Shock Absorber

If your car frequently carries dramatically different weights at different times, you might want to consider a **variable load shock absorber**. Either mechanically or electronically (by computer), the shock absorber responds differently to various weights carried in the car. The variable load shock absorber does this by first sensing a change in weight. It then changes the size of the piston's openings: larger and the ride is smoother, smaller and the ride is harsher.

Ball Joints and Bushings

Ball joints are the connecting joints of the steering and suspension systems. An integral part of both the steering and the suspension, ball joints allow the steering components to move up and down, as well as side to side, compensating for uneven road surfaces. As ball joints wear, you might experience a "sloppiness" or feeling of looseness in the steering as you drive.

One other suspension part that you may eventually need to replace during the lifetime of your car is a **bushing**. This metal or rubber lining helps to reduce wear between two parts by acting as a cushion. Bushings are not restricted to the suspension but are found throughout the car.

Ball joints are the connecting joints of the steering and suspension systems.

In an active suspension, a computer responds to many sensors that detect tiny changes in the movement of the vehicle's body and wheels.

❖

Active or "Road Smart" Suspension

In active suspensions, a series of sensors feeds information about vehicle speed, braking, and other handling characteristics to a computer. The computer then adjusts the ride (by altering the spring and shock absorber movements) for changing road conditions, thus enhancing ride comfort and handling. In the not-too-distant future, computers may direct the suspension components to adjust the load on each wheel. This will help the car to lean to the inside when rounding a curve, like a motorcycle does. Who knows? Someday computers may enable cars to walk up stairs.

Future cars may have computer-assisted suspension components that allow the car to lean into the curve, just like a motorcycle does.

It's Not Just Vanilla Anymore

Many of today's vehicles come with a variety of suspension choices, from a base system to off-road, from sport to touring. Each has its own distinctive comfort and handling characteristics. When looking at suspension features, first evaluate your own driving needs. Be sure you test drive a vehicle with the same suspension system that

Suspension System Choices

BASE   OFF-ROAD   TOURING

you will be buying. Test drive different types, but be sure that you really need the super-duper, more expensive suspension before you pay for it. If you're a speed-limit highway driver, you may be buying a feature that you will never take advantage of.

Making your car go the distance
Steering and Suspension Systems

Here are some tips to keep these systems in good working order.

✓ Check the power steering fluid level in the reservoir or have it checked about once a month, and top it off when necessary. The dipstick is usually located under the cap of the power steering pump.

Money-Saving Tip

"Front end work," a term that lumps together all repairs on the steering and suspension components, has traditionally been an area of high consumer dissatisfaction. If a technician recommends the replacement of steering or suspension components, ask the shop to show you what method is being used to determine wear. Often it is the manufacturer's specifications (tolerances) that determine excess wear, not the earlier method of shaking or moving a component. For this precise diagnosis a technician needs a sophisticated dial-indicator gauge.

Regularly check the power steering fluid level in the reservoir.

✔ If you have to add fluid every time you check the dipstick, there's probably a leak in the system. Have it inspected by a professional.

✔ When adding fluid, check your owner's manual for the correct type. Power steering and automatic transmission fluids are not interchangeable, and substitutions can cause serious problems.

✔ Have the suspension and steering components inspected and adjusted at manufacturer's recommended intervals. The rods, levers, and connectors wear with use and stretch with age. Proper inspection and adjustment will extend their useful life by many thousands of miles.

✔ Watch for signs of shock absorber wear, which can be detected by stepping down on one side of the bumper and then releasing it. If the car continues to bounce up and down more than three times, you probably have a worn shock absorber.

Signs of Shock Absorber Wear

More bounce than usual

Car dips forward when braking

Noise and bottoming out on bumps

Dark fluid on shock absorber

❖

✓ Some steering and suspension components are quick and easy to reach; others are not. Make sure your estimate indicates parts and labor costs, and then check around to see if the quoted price is reasonable.

Troubleshooting the Steering and Suspension Systems

Possible causes

Symptoms	Low power steering fluid	Slipping power steering belt	Faulty power steering pump	Wheel bearings	Worn/loose steering component/linkage	Lack of suspension/steering lubrication	Worn/loose suspension components (suspension arms/ball joints)	Worn shock absorbers, struts, bushings	Loose nuts and bolts in steering/suspension	Worn/broken springs	Wheels out of alignment
Car pulls to one side			●	●			●		●	●	●
Car hard to steer	●	●	●			●	●				
Looseness in steering					●				●		
Car vibrates at high speeds				●			●	●			●
Steering wheel shakes				●			●	●	●		
Growling noise	●		●	●							
Loud squealing noise		●									
Noises (thumps) in front end					●		●	●		●	
Body sways excessively in corners							●	●		●	
Car wanders over road					●		●	●	●		●

*Be certain to check tires and air pressure in tires before repairs to the suspension system are attempted.

12
Brakes

B rakes play a critical role in your safety. In this chapter you'll learn how brakes work, why they sometimes squeak and squeal, and whether you should be concerned if yours do. You'll learn what to look for if your brakes are about to let you down, and how you can avoid expensive brake component replacement with timely brake maintenance. Also covered are how anti-lock brakes and traction control work. ❖

The brake system

❖

Early cars had brakes only on the rear wheels. The systems were often inefficient, complex, and, not infrequently, hazardous to one's health. Brakes often experienced "**fading**," a terrifying condition in which the

Getting a ton or more of metal and rubber to roar down the road is only half the battle; prudence dictates that we also have a reliable way to stop it.

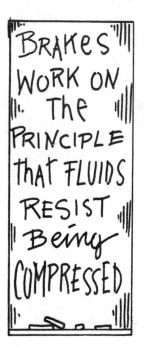

brakes failed completely as a result of overheating. Early brakes also required a lot of strength from the driver to stop the car.

How Brakes Work

Brake systems operate on all four wheels of the car and use brake fluid under pressure to stop the car when you step on the brake pedal.

Today's vehicles have a dual braking system; the front and the rear brakes operate separately. Here are the steps and components:

1. Brake fluid is stored in a metal or plastic container called a **master cylinder**, which is divided into two sections. Each section activates a separate set of brakes. If there is a leak in either one of the systems, a valve seals off the malfunctioning system from the healthy system. This

Brake components

❖

is to ensure that you will always be able to stop the car.

2. When you push on the brake pedal, brake fluid is forced out of the master cylinder through the **brake lines** to the brakes at each wheel.

The two types of brakes are **disc brakes** and **drum brakes**. Disc brakes are generally found in the front of a vehicle (where most of the braking is done), and drum brakes in the rear. Today, however, many vehicles have four-wheel disc brakes.

3. **Power brakes** use the power of the engine to assist braking. The power brake booster adds pressure to the brake fluid so that you don't need to exert as much pressure.

4. On most cars, the parking, or emergency, brake works on the rear brakes. When the parking brake is applied, the brake linings are forced against the drums until released. This keeps the car from moving after it has already stopped.

Drum Brakes

In a drum brake, a round metal container is attached to the turning wheel. Inside are two crescent-shaped pieces of metal called **brake shoes**. The shoes are backed with friction material called **brake linings**. The composition of this friction material is similar to that of a clutch disc: tough and heat-resistant.

WHEEL CYLINDER   BRAKE DRUM

BRAKE ADJUSTER   BRAKE LINING

SHOES

In a drum brake a round metal container is attached to the turning wheel. Inside are two crescent-shaped objects called brake shoes.

Between the two linings is a hollow tube called a **wheel cylinder**. Inside the wheel cylinder are two arms, called pistons. When you push on the brake pedal, brake fluid is forced through the brake lines and fills the wheel cylinder to capacity. This forces the pistons out against the linings, and the linings now rub against the inside of the drum. The resulting friction causes the drum and the wheel to slow down and eventually to stop. When the brake pedal is released, the fluid returns to the reservoir, and return springs bring the shoes back into their original positions. The shoes remain in this retracted position until the pedal is pushed again.

Disc Brakes

Disc brakes use the same principle as drum brakes but different mechanisms. A pair of kidney-shaped brake pads lined with friction material sit on either side of a metal disc called a **rotor**. The rotor is connected to the turning wheel. A **caliper**, a metal "fist" with one or two pistons in it, is attached to the brake pads. When you step on the brake pedal, the brake fluid is forced out of the master cylinder to the caliper. In the caliper, the brake fluid forces the pistons to squeeze the pads against the turning rotor. This causes the rotor and the wheel to slow and eventually stop.

With disc brakes, a pair of kidney-shaped brake pads backed with friction material sits on either side of a metal disc called a rotor. The rotor is connected to the turning wheel.

Brake warning light

Brake Warning Light

If a brake warning light flashes on the instrument panel even occasionally, it indicates trouble in the system. You could have a loss of brake fluid, a leak in the brake system, or air in the brake lines. Or it may simply mean that your rear or parking brakes need adjustment. Get the vehicle slowly and safely off the road, and have the system inspected by a professional as soon as possible. And always double-check to make certain you have fully released the parking brake before attempting to drive off.

Money-Saving Tip

Have brake fluid changed every two or three years, or every 30,000 miles (50,000 kilometers), whichever comes first. Brake fluid is subject to contamination by moisture, which can enter through the rubber brake lines that carry it. This caustic fluid deteriorates with age. When it does, it attacks the expensive brake components. Periodically replacing brake fluid will save you expensive brake component replacement in the future.

Early Warning System

You may hear a chirping noise coming from the front wheels, not when you're braking, but when the car is moving. If so, it is probably a "brake wear indicator" or sensor, a small piece of soft metal positioned so that it touches the surface of the rotor when the pad is ready to be replaced. It's saying, "Hey there! Your brake pads are low. Replace them now, before a routine maintenance item like brake pad replacement develops into the expensive replacement of major brake components!"

A brake wear indicator makes a high-pitched warning sound when the brake pads need replacement.

Anti-lock Brakes

Anti-lock brake systems (ABS) have been around since the late 1940s, but until recently, they weren't installed on anything you would have driven—unless you were a licensed commercial pilot. This computer-controlled automatic braking system helps you to steer around an obstacle while braking hard, even on slick surfaces.

Traction

❖

To understand how anti-lock brakes work, it's important to remember that the reason a moving car sticks to the road is because the car's tires turn. The turning of the tires against the road surface generates friction. We call that friction **traction**.

Now imagine that a child's ball rolls out in front of a moving car. How do most people respond? They stomp on the brake pedal. And what very often happens? The car skids because the brakes are applied with such force that they stop the tires from turning. This is called "wheel lock-up." No turning, no friction. No friction, no traction.

Now, traction's a good thing. (Unless, of course, you've been in an accident; that kind of traction is no fun.) Without traction, your one-ton-plus hunk of metal and rubber thinks it's parked.

The purpose of an anti-lock braking system is to avoid wheel lock-up and to allow the driver to maintain control. A computer receives messages from sensors located at the wheels. If a wheel is about to lock up, the computer automatically reduces the braking force at that wheel and then reapplies it when the wheel starts to turn again. The effect is similar to pumping the brakes, but at a rate much faster than most drivers ever could achieve.

◀ **No ABS**

◀ **With ABS**

Anti-lock brakes help you avoid wheel lock-up and allow you to maintain control of your vehicle.

❖

It's like having Mario Andretti driving your car for you at that moment. The car will not necessarily stop any quicker, but stability and steering control are maintained.

The correct way to use ABS in an emergency is to apply the brake pedal with what you feel is appropriate force and let the computer take over. You will probably sense the brake pedal vibrate and you may hear noises, or a dash light may indicate the ABS system has been activated. By the way, all ABS systems are designed so that the car will have normal (non-ABS assisted) braking should the ABS system fail.

Traction Control

Traction control is an adjunct to ABS that uses sophisticated electronics to help you stay on track even when the

Frequently asked questions

Q I just got new brakes, and they squeak. I asked about this and the repair shop said it's normal. Are they telling me the truth?

A Probably, but the condition isn't "normal," it's "common." Modern brake pads and linings are no longer made of asbestos (thanks to the EPA), but of tiny slivers of metal and other materials compressed together. These brake pads and linings are much harder than asbestos. They have excellent friction qualities, but, unfortunately, they often make noise.

The trick is to determine whether the noise is a problem or just an annoyance. Sometimes the sounds are the result of tiny variations in the surface of the pad. The newer type pads often don't conform as easily to the surface of the rotor. A squeak or squeal may be the result of vibrations. If you've had a new set of brake pads installed and are hearing this sound, have the brake work re-checked by the shop that did the work. They should be looking for loose parts.

Changes in temperature or changes in the moisture content of the atmosphere also affect friction characteristics that can set off a round of squeaking and squealing.

road is slick. A computer tracks input from wheel sensors that feed back information about the movement of the wheels. If the computer receives information that a wheel is about to slip, it automatically applies brakes to the problem wheel. It may also reduce engine power and make a change to the transmission gearing. Wheel slippage is eliminated, traction is restored, and the vehicle retains its grip.

MASTER CYLINDER
RESERVOIR

Check the brake fluid level in the master cylinder reservoir once a month, or have a professional check it for you.

❖

Making your car go the distance
Brake System

Here are some tips to help ensure that your brakes are responsive and reliable.

✓ Check or have the brake fluid level in the master cylinder reservoir checked once a month. Most cars have a translucent brake fluid reservoir that allows you to check the fluid level without opening the container. If the brake fluid is low on a regular basis, have the system professionally inspected as soon as possible.

✓ If you have to add brake fluid, wipe the top of the container with a clean cloth before opening.

A thorough brake inspection includes examination of the master cylinder, the brake lines, linings, rotors, drums, pads, calipers, and wheel cylinders.

❖

Contaminated brake fluid has been responsible for more than one instance of brake failure.

✓ Learn to recognize the signs of faulty brakes: brake noise (such as squeaking or grinding), a low or spongy feel to the brake pedal, rapid brake fluid loss, or a pulsating or vibrating brake pedal. Note: If you notice the brake fluid is disappearing on a regular basis, have the system professionally inspected as soon as possible.

Squeaking or grinding can indicate worn brakes.

✓ Have a professional check the brake system once a year. The technician should inspect all working parts and report what percentage of your brake pads and linings remain. They should be replaced when they still have about 25 to 30 percent of their friction material. Excess wear ruins rotors and drums, which greatly reduces braking efficiency and dramatically adds to repair costs.

✓ Brake pads and linings are "normal wear and tear" items. As the brake pads and linings get thinner, they have to travel farther to make contact with the rotor or drum, and braking action gradually diminishes. A periodic brake adjustment is often required to compensate on drum brakes. Disc brakes are self-adjusting.

✓ Be sure your regular brake service includes a parking brake inspection and adjustment when necessary. If the parking brake is working correctly, the car should not move forward easily in drive or first gear.

✓ Replace brake pads and linings with materials similar to the original equipment: have semi-metallic pads replaced with semi-metallic and non-metallic replaced with non-metallic. An occasional squeak or squeal that does not affect good braking is probably something you'll have to live with. *Note:* Have brakes inspected immediately if there is any change in the braking pattern.

✓ Brake service often includes shaving off a thin layer of metal from the rotor or drum to remove scratches and irregularities in their surface. This process is called **cutting** or **turning**, and there is a legal limit to how much metal can be removed. If the scratches or grooves are too deep, you may need to buy new rotors or drums. Brake components, no matter what kind, are always replaced in pairs.

✓ Ask for a written warranty or guarantee and read it over carefully. Ask questions about anything you do not fully understand.

✓ Wheel bearings are usually serviced when brake work is done. In some vehicles, wheel bearings are removed periodically and repacked with clean grease to extend the life of the working parts.

On most front-wheel drive vehicles, front wheel bearings are sealed at the factory. If they wear, they must be replaced, and they are always replaced in pairs. Read your owner's manual for specifics.

Troubleshooting the Brake System

Possible causes

Symptoms	Air in brake fluid	Low/contaminated brake fluid	Worn/glazed pads/linings	Grease/fluid on pads/linings	Pads/linings need adjustment	Defective master cylinder	Defective wheel cylinder/caliper	Faulty power brake booster	Warped brake disc/drum	Dirt in brake mechanism	Clogged/kinked/weak hoses and lines	Parking brake adjustment/rust	Computer-related (ABS)
Brake warning light on		●				●	●					●	●
Pedal hard (excess pedal effort)			●	●		●	●	●		●			
Pedal spongy	●					●							
Pedal sinks to floor	●				●	●	●						
Pedal vibrates/pulsates	●								●				
Noise when brakes applied			●		●				●	●			●
Brakes grab			●	●									
Brakes pull	●		●	●		●	●			●			
Brakes drag				●		●			●	●			
Parking brake inoperative												●	
ABS light on													●

13
Tires, Wheels, and Other Round Things

Your tires are the only direct contact your car has with the road. This chapter shows what you can do to make them perform better and last longer, including how to buy the right tires for your car at the best price. It also explains what wheel balancing, alignment, and rotation are and when they should be done. ❖

In 1900, the average family traveled about 200 miles a year. Today's family travels about 15,000.

Tires

❖

In combination with your car's suspension, steering, and brakes, tires help to keep your car on the road and going in the direction you want. Four contact patches that are no bigger than the size of your hand are the only connection between your car and the road. Tires also provide a nice pillow of air in the form of a spongy rubber shoe worn by your car's metal feet, the wheels.

Today's tires are constructed of a combination of fabrics and materials that isolate you from the jolting impact of the bumps, stones, potholes, and washboard surfaces over which you travel. They are designed to provide a compromise between comfort, good road handling, and long wear. Their predecessors, on the other hand, endlessly jiggled and jostled their passenger's spines and dentures and were, according to many accounts, one of the most expensive and least reliable of all car parts. Deeply rutted roads filled with nails left by decades of horseshoes made two and three punctures on a journey commonplace. For many years, tires were drivers' weakest link.

In the early days, cars ran on tires of narrow solid rubber, and the ride was uncomfortable and unstable. It was common to see cars in ditches along the side of the road. A car was about as predictable as a skittish horse, and it would be a while before the term "steady as she goes" could accurately be applied to automobiles.

As cars grew larger and heavier and engine speeds increased, they needed greater stability in the form of a bigger, broader footprint. Tire manufacturers responded with the development of wider balloon tires. The chances of a car's staying on the road improved dramatically. The chances improved even more with the addition of "grooves"—channels cut in the smooth rubber of the tread (the part that comes in contact with the road).

How Tires Work

Grooves are channels cut into the tire. They provide drainage for water.

Theoretically, the best design for a tire would be a wide smooth one, with no grooves or indentations. This design would provide the maximum surface for contacting the road. If grooves are made in this smooth surface, the amount of tire surface in direct contact with the road is reduced. But the grooves provide drainage for water, mud, and snow so that secure contact with the road can be maintained. Smooth or grooved tires? The answer is both. And the compromise between the two dictates the construction of every modern tire.

Mr. Goodyear perfected his tire by mistake.

❖

Early Tire Development

Tires owe a debt to Mrs. Goodyear. Her husband, Charles, experimented with tire-making for more than five years. His obsession led his family to public ridicule, poverty, and to debtor's prison. He finally promised his wife that he would give up his quest. But in a weak moment, while Mrs. Goodyear was away from home, he broke his word and began experimenting with one element he had not tried before. Unfortunately, or fortunately as it turned out, Mrs. Goodyear returned home unexpectedly. Goodyear threw the mixture in the oven to avoid detection. Sometime later he retrieved his concoction and discovered that heat had been just the thing it needed. His kitchen experiment would eventually produce the material that would be the foundation for modern tires, a solid substance with plenty of give: rubber.

Tire components

❖

You've Come a Long Way, Baby

Great advances have been made in tire construction since Mr. Goodyear's domestic experiments. Here are the basic components of today's tires:

1. Steel wheels are attached to the hubs located at the end of each axle by heavy metal bolts called lugs. The lugs are secured by lug nuts.

2. A "**bead**," thin strips of metal wound together into a narrow ring, provides an airtight grip on the wheels.

3. "**Plies**" are pieces of material that are attached to the bead. It is the material of the ply and the angle at which the threads or "cords" of the plies meet each other that determine the tire's construction category.

4. Bias-ply tires have plies that meet each other on the "diagonal." In other words, at an angle of roughly 35 to 40 degrees.

5. Radial tires, which are standard equipment on most newer cars, have plies that meet each other at right angles, that is, 90 degrees. Radials provide a more comfortable ride and contain strips of metal or fiberglass which make the tires stiffer, improve their cornering capability, and extend their useful life.

6. Wheel bearings are metal doughnuts with many tiny steel balls, called ball bearings, inside. They extend the life of the axles and contribute significantly to proper road handling through smooth steering and braking. They distribute the weight and turning force of the axle shaft. They are found where the axle joins the wheel.

Reading Tires

In order to help consumers choose from the numerous tire models that are available, the government has developed a uniform rating system that includes three categories: traction, resistance to heat, and resistance to wear. This rating is stamped on the side of all passenger car tires (not truck or snow tires), along with symbols that indicate the tire's size and type of construction. The illustration on the following page shows you how to interpret this information and can help you choose a quality product and correct replacement tire for your car.

1. a & b. The brand name and tire model.

2. Tire's type of construction.

3. Maximum Air Pressure. This is *not* the recommended inflation pressure for your tires. That number is specific to your vehicle. See below for more about tire pressure.

4. DOT and the letters and numbers following are the tire's identification number, useful if the tire is recalled. The last three digits, 035, indicate the week and the last digit of the year the tire was made. This tire was manufactured in the third week of 1995. When buying tires, look for those tires that have been manufactured within the last year.

5. Tire size and general type.

a. P stands for passenger vehicle.

b. The number 195 tells you how wide the tire is. It's measured in millimeters.

c. The number 60 indicates how tall the tire is. It is

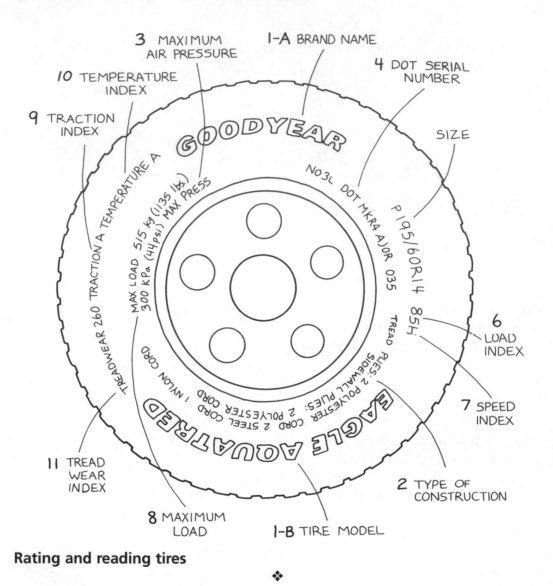

3 MAXIMUM AIR PRESSURE

1-A BRAND NAME

10 TEMPERATURE INDEX

4 DOT SERIAL NUMBER

9 TRACTION INDEX

SIZE

GOODYEAR

TEMPERATURE A

515 kg (1135 lbs.) MAX PRESS

300 KPa (44 psi) MAX PRESS

MAX LOAD

TRACTION A

No 3L DOT MKR4 AJOR 035

P 195/60R14

TREADWEAR 260

1 NYLON CORD

85H

6 LOAD INDEX

TREAD PLIES: 2 POLYESTER CORD 2 STEEL CORD

SIDEWALL PLIES: 2 POLYESTER CORD

7 SPEED INDEX

11 TREAD WEAR INDEX

EAGLE AQUATRED

2 TYPE OF CONSTRUCTION

8 MAXIMUM LOAD

1-B TIRE MODEL

Rating and reading tires

❖

represented as a ratio of the tire's height divided by its width. The tires with taller sidewalls (ratios of 60 or 70) are often found on passenger cars. Tires with shorter sidewalls (ratios of 50) are more often found on sports cars and are called performance tires. They offer improved steering response and road feel. The drawback is that passengers often experience a harsher ride.

d. The letter R indicates the way in which the tire is constructed. R stands for radial ply. All new passenger cars and light trucks are equipped with radials, and most replacement tires are radials.

e. The number 14 indicates the wheel diameter this tire fits, as measured in inches.

6. The load index indicates the maximum weight that this tire can carry at its maximum speed rating.

7. The letter H indicates the tire's speed rating. H indicates a speed rating up to 130 mph (210 km/h). The top ratings are W which indicates a speed rating of 168 mph (269 km/h), and Z which has an unlimited speed rating.

8. "Tread wear" rates how long a tire is expected to last. Ratings start at 100 and go up to 500. In general, a tire with a 200 rating will last twice as long as a tire with a 100.

It's important to remember that tire wear is also determined by tire maintenance (inflation) and how you drive. High-speed driving causes more heat and thus, more wear. Where you drive is also a factor (substandard roads take their toll on rubber).

9. "Traction" followed by a letter grade of A to C, rates the tire's ability to stop on a wet road surface. C is the lowest measure. The important word here is wet. This index does not reveal the tire's capabilities on a dry pavement or any other type of surface. While it is important, it should not be the only factor influencing a buying decision.

10. "Temperature" grades the tire's ability to withstand and dissipate heat. A is the highest grade; C is the lowest.

All-Season versus Mud and Snow Tires

Conventional treads provide good traction on dry roads. All-season tires last longer than snow tires and still do a reasonably good job of handling bad weather road conditions. If you live in an area where the average snow and ice accumulation is marginal, all-season tires can save you some money by limiting you to one set of tires.

The tread on a mud and snow tire has especially deep grooves, which are specifically designed to dig down and make contact with the road surface below. This aggressive tread works great on ice and snow, but it wears faster on dry roads than a conventional tread does.

Studded tires have metal studs embedded in them.

CONVENTIONAL   ALL-SEASON   MUD AND SNOW   STUDDED SNOW   CHAINS

Today's tire choices

❖

While not legal in all states, they offer even more traction in the toughest of conditions.

Chains may also be an option if you live in an area where you get heavy snow, but only occasionally. They cannot be driven at highway speeds on dry roads. Although chains are easier to install than they were years ago, putting chains on still means getting out of the car in the snow and crawling around on your hands and knees.

Money-Saving Tip

Research tells us that as many as half the cars on the road have at least one tire that is seriously underinflated. That's bad news, since the single largest reason for tire failure (blowouts) is underinflation. Furthermore, underinflated tires do not handle as well, take longer to stop, and wear faster. Even a small degree (4 psi) of underinflation can decrease a tire's life by as much as 10 percent. Checking tire pressure can protect both your safety and your pocketbook.

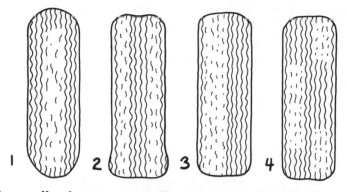

Tires tell tales: 1. overinflation, 2. underinflation, 3. tread wear on one side only, 4. erratic tread wear.

❖

1. Overinflation—When a tire has too much air (is overinflated), only its middle section touches the road surface. The tire's sides pull up and away from the road and only a small amount of tread makes contact with the road. There is excessive wear in the middle.

2. Underinflation—When a tire does not have enough air (is underinflated), its sides sag and puff out, and its middle section pulls up and away from the pavement. Only a small portion of the tread makes contact with the road. The tire will show wear on the edges.

3. Tread wear on one side only—An irregular tread wear pattern on the tire, with wear accelerated on one side only, is often an indicator of alignment problems.

4. Tire is worn erratically—If the tire is worn erratically (a pattern that is referred to as cupping, or scalloping) it may be that the wheel is out of balance, or the shock absorbers or ball joints may be worn.

Special Spare Tires

Small or "doughnut" spare tires are good at doing what they're designed for, that is, saving storage space. They are to be driven at a speed no greater than the number stamped on the side of the tire and must be replaced with a standard spare as soon as possible. As an added bonus, you don't have to be Man Mountain Dean to get it out of the trunk if you do have to change a flat tire.

1

2

3

4

Checking tire pressure is an easy do-it-yourself inspection.

Run-flat Tires

Run-flat tires can be driven for limited distances even while deflated. They have been specially reinforced to retain their shape and support a vehicle's weight so that the driver retains full control, even with the tire at zero pressure.

Making your car go the distance
Tires and Wheels

Maintaining tires is as easy as brushing your teeth. Really.

✓ Check tire pressure once a month and before going on a trip. Don't forget to check the spare—even spares can lose air. And don't assume that the air pressure in your tires is correct because they look okay.

✓ Use a good quality tire gauge. Tire gauges come in two basic types: pencil and dial. The dial gauges cost more, but they are a little easier to read. Just be sure the one you buy can measure inflation up to 60 pounds since the smaller spare tires usually need this higher pressure.

✓ Check tires when they are cold, i.e., the car should be standing for a few hours before you check them. As you drive, the tire temperature rises and so does the pressure. Warm tires will give an inaccurate reading. Follow these steps:

1. Locate the automaker's recommended tire pressure for your car. Ignore the number printed on the tire; it is generally too high for normal use. Look in the glove compartment or inside one of the doorjambs for a label with the words "Cold Tire Pressure" followed by the letters "F" for front and "R" for rear.

2. Locate the valve stem on the tire and remove its protective cap.

3. Apply the tire gauge to the valve stem at a right

angle and push firmly. If using a pencil-type gauge, be sure to push the nylon measurement tab all the way in before applying it to the valve stem.

You will probably hear a whoosh of air, which is normal. (You are not letting all the air out of your tires—unless you continue to push on the pin, in which case air will escape.) The firmer and more directly you apply the gauge, the less air will leak out. The nylon tab will pop out of the bottom of the gauge, revealing a number that indicates the air pressure in pounds per square inch. If you're using a dial type, the needle will move from zero to a number.

4. If your pressure is too low, drive to a nearby service station to add air. Do not trust the service station's gauge; most are notoriously inaccurate. That's why you have your own gauge.

Checking Tread Wear

Check tread wear with an inexpensive tread depth indicator or an even less expensive penny. Replace tires when the tread has worn to approximately $\frac{1}{16}$ inch (1.6 mm). Don't wait until you need an immediate replacement. You increase the risk of tire failure and may miss out on buying the best quality tires on sale.

✓ Today's tires also have wear indicators in them called **wear bars**. A wear bar is a thin bald strip that appears across two or more treads when the tread has worn to about a $\frac{1}{16}$ inch (1.6 mm) depth. Keep an eye out for these and when they appear, begin looking for replacement tires.

✓ Watch for tears, bulges, or abnormal lumps in the tread or sidewall. If you find any of these defects, have the tire checked immediately and replaced, if necessary.

✓ To ensure longer life and even wear, tires should be rotated every 8,000 miles (13,000 kilometers).

Check tread depth by sticking a penny in a groove. If you can see the top of Abe's head (or all of the Queen's crown), it's time for a new set of tires.

Today's tires sport indicators called wear bars.

RADIAL

You'll find the tire rotation pattern for your car in your owner's manual. Here is one common pattern.

Front tires typically wear faster than rear ones, because the weight in the car shifts forward when you stop. Front wheels also feel the impact of steering, and in the case of front-wheel drive, driving.

✓ If you switch to snow or alternate tires during the year, make sure the tires are marked as they are removed from the car. Their position on the car should be written on the tire with chalk or an easily readable, non-permanent marker.

Wheel Alignment

Alignment has to do with the angle at which the tires meet the road. For a car to handle well, the tires need to sit slightly tilted to the road surface. It takes a trained technician with a computerized alignment machine to create an angle that best accommodates these needs.

✓ To ensure longer tire life, have a wheel alignment check whenever your tires are being serviced. If there is a deviation from manufacturer specifications, corrections are made to the camber (the inward or outward tilt of a wheel), caster (the forward or rearward tilt of a wheel when viewed from the side), and toe (a measure of two wheels' parallel alignment; "**toe in**" is analogous to a pigeon-toed condition, and "**toe out**" is analogous to a duck-footed condition).

✓ The frequency of a wheel alignment check depends on the type of driving you do and the road conditions, but once a year is a good rule of thumb. Rough roads, gravity force starts, quarter horse stops, and parking on the curb instead of next to it will increase your need for more frequent alignment.

✓ Most cars today (all those with independent rear suspensions) require an alignment of all four wheels. If a technician speaks about a front-wheel alignment, be wary. If you are uncertain what type of rear

Examples of alignment: a. excessive camber, b. caster side view, c. incorrect toe

❖

suspension your vehicle has, ask your regular service provider.

✓ A good alignment technician always checks for worn steering and suspension parts and for dragging brakes before doing an alignment.

✓ Make certain your tires are properly inflated before having them aligned.

✓ Make certain each wheel alignment check and any required adjustments are noted on the repair order. There may only be two checks done if the caster was preset by the manufacturer. Ask that each adjustment be explained to you.

If no corrections are needed after an alignment inspection, the charge is generally less than that for inspecting and making adjustments.

✓ To avoid warped rotors, insist that a torque wrench be used to tighten all lug nuts and that the wrench be set to manufacturer's specifications.

Wheel Balancing

Wheel balancing compensates for a tire's unevenness (they look round but they're not). Small metal weights are attached to the wheels to make them turn evenly. There are two popular ways to balance tires—static, with the wheels off the car, and dynamic, with the wheels on. The preferred method is dynamic balancing because it allows for the influence of the brakes and suspension components.

LEAD WEIGHTS

When wheels are balanced, small metal weights are attached to them to make the wheels turn evenly.

✔ Have your wheels balanced whenever having new tires mounted or whenever tires are removed from their rims. If you remove a tire simply to look at something else, the weights remain untouched, and the tire shouldn't need to be balanced.

✔ Wheel bearings are packed with grease, providing a lubricating cushion. Have wheel bearings repacked whenever your owner's manual suggests, or more frequently if you do a lot of off-road driving. Wheel bearings that are sealed at the factory should be replaced in pairs if they fail.

Replacing Tires

✔ Replacement tires should be the same size, design, and whenever possible, brand as the original tires.

✔ When buying replacement tires, take the time to learn more about them. Don't pay for tire qualities that you won't use.

✔ Make certain the price quoted for replacement tires includes wheel balancing and installation.

✔ Buying new tires does not necessarily mean that you need a wheel alignment. If the old tires were wearing uniformly, it's likely the new ones will also.

✔ Ask about written warranties before you buy. The longer, the better. And keep all documentation in a safe place.

Frequently asked questions

Hydroplaning occurs when a layer of water forms between the tire and the road surface.

Q What really happens when a car hydroplanes?

A **Hydroplaning** is a scary driving condition that occurs when a layer of water forms between the tire and the road surface. The treads cannot push the water through fast enough. The tire climbs up on a wedge of water and suddenly looses contact with the road. Traction and control go right out the window. Tire grooves can push only so much water through them before they fill. Sufficient tread, the correct tire pressure, and slowing your car's speed as you approach large puddles helps the vehicle regain traction by allowing the grooves more time to work.

Tire and Wheel Runout

Among the ills a tire or a wheel may suffer is **radial** or **lateral runout**. Radial runout is the difference between the low and high points on the tread of the tire. Lateral runout is the wobble of the tire or wheel. Both irregularities can be determined with a runout gauge and matched against manufacturer's specifications. If the runout is excessive, the remedy may be as simple as cleaning and remounting the tire. If that doesn't solve the problem, the tire and/or wheel should be replaced.

Troubleshooting Tires and Wheels

Symptoms	Possible causes				
	Incorrect tire pressure	Mismatched tires	Faulty tire/bent wheel	Wheels out of balance	Hard driving, hard braking
Car pulls or drifts to one side	●	●			
Abnormal/excessive tire wear	●			●	●
Shaking, vibration in steering wheel	●		●	●	
Squealing in corners	●				
Thumping from tire/wheel			●	●	

14
Choosing and Dealing with Service Providers

This chapter will help you to choose an honest and competent repair shop, and give you tips on how to deal with repair personnel. It will also teach you how to protect yourself against dishonesty, incompetence, and overcharging. You'll learn how to describe a symptom so that you have a better chance of getting the repair done right the first time. You'll also learn what you can do if it isn't right the first time. ❖

Wouldn't it be wonderful if every time your car broke down, a fairy god-mechanic appeared and, with a wave of her magic ratchet, turned your lemon into a dream car? Unfortunately, mechanics in the real world are of the mere mortal variety. If you own a car, sooner or later you are going to have to pick one to work on it.

Choosing a repair shop is a task most consumers approach with all the fear, loathing, and paranoia they can muster. It doesn't have to be that way. The repair shops of this world are not all out to get us. But just as in any other profession, their ranks include the good, the bad, and the indifferent.

To be sure, there are a number of incompetent and unskilled technicians. In many states, all those with a rusty screwdriver and the inclination can call themselves technicians and offer to operate on your car. For the few states that do require certification or licensing

You probably won't find yourself a fairy god-mechanic, but you can find honest, competent service professionals.

Do some research before you choose a repair shop.

of technicians, the requirements to qualify are usually minimal. As cars become more sophisticated, the situation worsens.

To complicate matters further, there are some in the field who, although they are skilled, lack scruples. Nevertheless, it's important that we don't lump all auto repair personnel in the same category. There are still a lot of technicians who are skilled and honest, and it is possible for you to find one. You don't even need a degree in auto repair, just common sense and the willingness to do some detective work.

Word of Mouth

When stalking a good repair shop, word of mouth is probably the best method. Ask your friends, relatives, co-workers, and insurance agents where they take their cars for servicing. Finding a qualified and honest technician can be just that easy. Use your common sense before acting on their recommendations. Just because Uncle Joe tells you he got a real good deal from See-U-Soon Auto Repair when they changed the oil in his car, it doesn't mean you should rush right down there and have your ailing transmission fixed. Even though the technicians at See-U-Soon may be wizards at changing oil, it could be that they wouldn't know a transmission if it crashed through the roof and landed with a bang in the garage bay.

Ask questions. What kind of work was done on Uncle Joe's car? Did the repair shop do just the work requested or did they make additional repairs? Did they exceed the estimate? If so, was there a valid reason and was Joe notified first? Is Uncle Joe known for his good judgment, or does he own 50 acres of swamp land in Florida? These are some of the questions that will get you the answers you need to make an intelligent decision.

Don't make the common mistake of restricting your choice to those shops closest to your home. A shop within walking distance is a great convenience, but should your car break down because Near-Your-House Fix-It didn't do the job right, you could find yourself a long, long way from home.

Other Methods

Although personal referral is one of the best ways to find a good technician, it is not the only way. There are other sources of this information. Automobile clubs, in addition to providing emergency road service, are also knowledgeable about good repair shops in your area. They often have lists which identify auto repair facilities that meet their standards of consistent, high-quality repair work and service. Consult your phone book. Shops with auto club approval usually mention that fact in their ads. Or call the auto clubs in your area for information.

Check the Shop's Reputation

Before you take your car into a new shop, don't forget to call the Consumer Complaint Division of your attorney general's office or the Better Business Bureau in your area. They won't recommend a technician or shop, but they will tell you if the one you're considering has unresolved complaints filed against it.

Don't Wait

It's best not to wait until you are in the vulnerable position of needing major repair work to try out a new shop or technician. Bring the car in first for a minor repair or routine maintenance job, such as an oil change or tire rotation. On that first visit, give the service area the

Today's cars require sophisticated diagnostic equipment to make repairs and to perform scheduled service properly.

❖

"once over." Is it reasonably organized and clean? Or does it look like it's been stirred with a large spoon? Does it have computerized diagnostic tools? Or is the technician equipped with a large wrench, a rusty screwdriver, and little else?

Black Box Magic

"Black boxes," which run everything from computerized ignitions to air temperature control, have replaced many mechanical parts. A shop doesn't have to look like a hangar out of *Star Wars*, but it must have the manuals and equipment needed to work on your computerized car. At a minimum, it must have modern engine analyzing equipment. These diagnostic computers check major engine components and their functions. They then give a printout that indicates whether each system is working properly, pinpointing what is wrong, or what needs further examination. A good shop should be willing to discuss its equipment and show you how it works. Keep in mind that even the most sophisticated diagnostic equipment needs a properly trained technician to run it.

While some of the smaller shops do great work, they can't afford the computerized machines necessary for more complex technical repairs and adjustments. They may be forced to begin blindly switching parts until they stumble onto the right one.

Intermittent Problems

One of the most frustrating consequences of computerized cars occurs when the problem symptom happens only occasionally or disappears when the technician drives the car. These intermittent problems often reduce the fix to a guess. There are, however, devices similar to flight recorders which can be attached to the car's computer while it is being driven. When the problem occurs, the device registers and stores the data for analysis later by the technician. Unfortunately, not all problems fall within the scope of these devices.

Your car may not cooperate when you want it to exhibit a problem.

Training Credentials

Quality workmanship, as well as parts, are major considerations when choosing a repair shop. Are the people who work on your car qualified and well trained, or did they just do their first oil change this morning?

All car manufacturers sponsor training programs and technical clinics for their technicians on an ongoing basis. They may also have their own certification programs. Certified technicians have passed demanding written and hands-on tests in different categories.

The National Institute for Auto Service Excellence (ASE) also certifies technicians through a series of eight written tests, each covering a different system of the car. Technicians must also have two years of hands-on work experience and be recertified every five years. Obviously, neither type of certification is a guarantee of competence, nor does it say anything about a technician's ethics. Still, certification is an indication of professionalism and certainly is better than nothing at all. Look for plaques on the shop's wall showing names and dates of certified technicians, or you may want to specifically ask to see a technician's credentials. Some of a shop's technicians may not be certified or may not be certified in all eight categories.

Rapport on Repairs

An equally important consideration in choosing a repair facility is attitude. Initial encounters should leave you feeling *comfortable* with the way you were treated. Were you listened to? Were you believed? Were you treated with respect and courtesy? Was the service writer or technician patient and did they act interested? Did she or he ask you pertinent questions that helped you to communicate about the problem that prompted your visit? Were they helpful? If you and your service provider cannot establish a rapport on repairs, chances are the relationship won't last for long. A long-term association with a single repair shop or technician is the best way for them to get to know you and your car.

If you're still waiting for the fairy god-mechanic to appear, forget it. Start looking for the next best thing—a fair and good technician. You could turn your grim tales of automotive woe into stories that end with you happily driving off into the sunset.

Specialists versus General Practitioners

Just as the medical world is full of specialists—doctors who only work on hearts, or ears, or feet—so, too, is the automotive world. The dealerships and independent repair shops that work only on a few makes of cars are most likely to have the trained technicians and updated

Just as the medical world has specialists and general practitioners, so too are there automotive shops which specialize in car makes or repair problems.

technical information that it takes to work on today's computerized vehicles.

When it comes to certain items, such as tires, a specialist may be less expensive than an independent shop or dealership. High volume usually allows the specialty retailer to charge less and still make a profit. Call each and compare their prices. Always be sure that the prices you are comparing are for items of the same quality. If the specialty shop is using parts of inferior quality, those big savings in time and money may not be much of a bargain.

Guarantees

And finally, is the work guaranteed? Does the guarantee cover parts and labor? How long is the coverage in effect? A common practice is to guarantee work for 90 days. Is there anything you must do to keep the guarantee in force?

Keep in mind that there are two types of guarantees in the automotive business—the "property line guarantee" and an authentic guarantee. The property line guarantee is the one where, after the repairs have been completed, you get to the end of their property line, and they guarantee they never want to see you again! The authentic guarantee is the one that guarantees if the job is not done right the first time, the shop is accountable. They listen to you, believe you, and do their best to make the repair right.

Assemble as much information about your car as you can before you visit the repair shop. Be prepared.

❖

Dealing with a Service Provider

Finding a good repair shop is essential, but it is not enough to ensure good car care. Make a maintenance log out of a spiral-bound notebook small enough to fit in the glove compartment or buy one in a store for a few dollars and change it to fit your needs. Record everything that happens to your car, for example, when you add fluids, oil, coolant, brake fluid, power steering fluid, and how much. Be specific. Just noting that oil was added isn't specific enough for you to track accurately. Record how much oil is added and its weight along with the date and the mileage (kilometers). Mark down which belts are changed, what filters are replaced, whether the front brakes or rear brakes are worked on, and any repairs that are made.

In the same notebook, keep track of your fuel economy. It's like keeping your finger on your car's pulse. A decrease in fuel economy over a short period of time is a sign that all is not well and will signal internal changes that may require simple adjustments or repairs to normalize them. If you record a drop of 10 percent in fuel economy over several fill-ups, bring it to the attention of your service provider.

Together with your manufacturer's service schedule, an up-to-date maintenance log is your best protection against unnecessary maintenance.

You are in a far more powerful position to help the technician diagnose a problem if you've been keeping accurate records. Keeping records may seem like a pain in the neck at first, but after a while, it will be like brushing your teeth, a habit so ingrained that you would be uncomfortable not doing it.

When used in conjunction with your manufacturer's schedule of service, an up-to-date maintenance log is also helpful in avoiding unnecessary maintenance and repairs. If someone tries to sell you a tire rotation in addition to the work you've requested, but you know your tires were rotated 2,000 miles (3,200 kilometers) ago and they're not due for rotation for another 5,500 miles

Warning! Do not assume that scheduled maintenance will automatically fix a problem. If you went to your doctor for your annual checkup and you had been having severe headaches for more than a month, would you expect the doctor to discover the problem without your communicating the symptoms? No, you'd need to carefully describe where the pain was, how often it occurred, and other specific circumstances that might shed some light on the problem. In the same way, when you bring your car in for scheduled service and there is a performance problem, be sure to tell your service provider about it. Supply as many pertinent details as you can. Doing this faithfully will go a long way toward keeping you out of the shop until the next scheduled service.

Use your five senses to detect as many symptoms as possible.

(8,800 kilometers), you'll be able to say, "no thanks." Make a mental note to see if it happens again the future. Anyone can make a mistake, but a consistent pattern of attempts to oversell is a sure sign of greed and dishonesty.

Studies show that millions of dollars are lost every year because of misdiagnosed car problems. But you can keep this from happening to you. Just as technicians are not fairy godmothers, they are also not magicians or psychics or even private detectives. Before your technician can diagnose or fix the problem, he or she needs to know what symptoms have brought you and your car to the repair shop.

You can save time, money, and frustration by taking the time to clearly explain the symptoms or conditions that brought you to the service facility. Make sure the repair shop has all the information that you have. After all, who knows your car better than you do? You may not know what's wrong with it, but you do know when something is wrong with it.

Describing Symptoms

Using your five senses—hearing, sight, smell, taste, and touch—is the key to explaining your car's troubles to the technician and getting them solved.

Cars in pain do complain—often loudly.

Your car may exhibit symptoms of ill health in the way it handles or "feels" to you. Does it pull to the left or the right?

Hearing: Noise is one of the more common ways your car will let you know it is not happy. Clicks, clunks, hisses, squeaks, squeals, rumbles, roars—yes, cars in pain do complain, but in their own language. Any of these sounds (or other unusual noises your car may create) could mean your car is heading for a breakdown or a repair. If the sound persists, you need to get the car inspected. Isolate the sound. Is it coming from the front, rear, left, right, under the hood, inside the dash, in a wheel well, from the engine?

Touch: Does the car vibrate, shimmy, shake, sputter, surge, hesitate, stall, or continue running after you turn off the ignition? Is the car hard to steer or does the steering feel loose or sloppy? When you press the brake pedal, does it feel spongy or too hard? Does the pedal slowly sink to the floor after you've stopped?

The vocabulary of your ailing car

Is your dashboard trying to tell you something?

Watch for leaks and learn to identify their sources.

Cars can be quite odorous, especially when they are trying to get your attention.

All right, all right, so we've taken a little poetic license on the fifth sense. Do not taste any automotive fluids or let any fluid touch an open sore or cut.

Sight: Are your dashboard warning lights illuminated or flickering? Is the needle of any gauge out of its normal range? If so, you may have a problem with your battery, alternator, brakes, engine temperature, or oil pressure. Watch, too, for other signs of a problem, such as a leak. To identify where a leak is coming from, slide a piece of cardboard under the car and check it after a few hours. Note the source of the leak—front, rear, middle, left, right, a nearby garage shelf? Keep in mind that many leaks only occur under pressure at highway speeds.

What color is the leaking fluid? Brownish-black oil is either engine oil or steering fluid. A thick black ooze might be manual transmission fluid. A reddish, oily film is probably automatic transmission fluid. Coolant is generally green, pink, or yellow. Air conditioning discharge is clear.

Smell: If you have a leak, you might want to touch your finger to the spot on the ground and sniff the fluid. Most people can recognize the smell of gasoline. Coolant smells sweet. The smell of burning rubber may indicate overheated brakes or clutch. A sick catalytic converter often announces itself with the smell of rotten eggs.

Taste: If you have licked, nibbled, or eaten any part of your car for any reason, you probably need more help than a technician will be able to give you.

The Three Cs: Changes, Conditions, and Communications

Remember the three Cs when explaining your car's trouble symptoms.

1. Change is often the first sign of a car problem. Does your car drink more fluids lately, such as gas, oil, coolant, transmission or brake fluid? Has your car suddenly become different in the way it handles or sounds? If it has always had a rattle in the rear end that sounds like your Uncle Harry trying to get out of the closet, you probably don't need to worry about it. But if you're driving down the road, and all of a sudden you hear a loud rattle, and it's getting worse by the minute, then you will probably want to have it checked. At least check the trunk. It could be a loose jack, or it really might be Uncle Harry.

2. Conditions: Under what conditions does the particular symptom occur? When you first start the car or after it has warmed up? When it's raining? When it's cold? Only when the heater is on? Only in first gear? Only on Tuesdays? When you're braking? Coasting? Accelerating?

3. Communications: After you've figured out as much as you can about what, how, when, and where your car's annoying symptom occurs, you must accurately communicate that information to your technician. Write everything down and give all the details. You might also want to tape a copy of the symptoms to the steering wheel. The person you talk to may not be the one who works on your car.

Here is an example of what you need to give your technician before anyone begins working on your car. Note these essential elements: (1) symptoms—as defined by the five senses and the three Cs above; (2) a telephone number where you can be reached; and (3) request for an estimate. The most technical term in the following letter

Remember the three Cs.

Dear Technician:

When I'm driving uphill at about 40 miles per hour (65 kilometers per hour), a whining sound comes from under the hood of my car which sounds like a big mosquito, then the car immediately stalls. It only does this on warm days (temperature above 50° F /10° C) and only after the car has been running for at least 15 minutes. After waiting at least a half hour, I am able to restart the car, at which time a big cloud of black smoke blows out of the tailpipe. Please call me at 555-1111 after your diagnosis to let me know how much you estimate the work will cost, if it will be more than $50. Thank you.

Sincerely,

Hope Itzminor

Garage-ese 101

Here are a few terms to help you describe your car's symptoms to a technician. (Turn to the glossary on page 214 to really improve your fluency in garage-ese.)

Engine Performance Terms

Afterfire—engine continues to fire after the vehicle has been turned off

Backfire—loud popping sound from the engine or tailpipe

Cuts out—irregular and complete loss of power

Dieseling—see *Afterfire*

Engine run on—see *Afterfire*

Fast idle—engine runs too fast

Hesitation—a pause or momentary lack of power

Miss—engine runs at speed erratically and unevenly

Power loss—engine continues to run but at dramatically reduced speed

Rough idle—slight engine vibration to severe shaking at a stop

Sluggish—power is less than normal, acceleration not as crisp as usual

Stall—engine dies completely

Stumble—engine starts to die and kicks back in before stalling

Surge—vehicle speeds up and slows down with no change in accelerator pedal pressure

Handling Terms

Bottoming—bottom of car scrapes the ground

Brake drag—brakes do not release completely

Brake fade—brakes take longer to stop the vehicle

Pitch—vehicle dives forward upon braking, or sideways upon cornering

Play—too much looseness in the steering wheel
Pull—vehicle strains to one side when braking
Shimmy—tires and steering wheel shake
Sway—vehicle continues to bounce after going over bump
Vibrate—vehicle shakes
Wander—vehicle drifts from side to side

is "tailpipe," proof that you don't need to study technical engineering to communicate satisfactorily to your technician.

Describe—Don't Diagnose

The second and last thing to remember about communications is: Describe—don't diagnose. If you had a stomachache, you wouldn't ask your doctor to remove your appendix, would you? No. You'd say you had a pain in your abdomen and that you were running a fever. The doctor would decide on the remedy.

The same is true of cars and technicians. If your car stalls and your neighbor tells you that when she had the exact same problem last month, the technician had to replace her car's fuel injectors, that doesn't mean you should walk into your service station and ask your technician to replace the fuel injectors. Your car might only need a minor adjustment or it may need something entirely different. *Tell the technician what your car is doing.* Describe the symptoms and let the technician make the diagnosis. The next time you have to visit the repair shop, make a checklist of your car's symptoms; see the sample checklist on the following page.

The troubleshooting charts included in this book are not intended to be exhaustive lists of problems or their causes. The charts are instead designed to familiarize you with some of the more common troublemakers. For

Symptoms Checklist

Check as many symptoms as necessary.

1. WHAT IS VEHICLE DOING?　　**Description**

☐ Noise　　_____

☐ Odor　　_____

☐ Visual　　_____

☐ Performance　　_____

☐ Handling　　_____

2. WHERE DOES IT COME FROM?

☐ Outside Car

　　☐ Engine compartment　　☐ Under the vehicle

　　☐ Left front　　　　　　　☐ Left rear

　　☐ Right front　　　　　　☐ Right rear

　　☐ Center

☐ Inside Car

　　☐ Instrument panel

　　☐ Seat　　　☐ Roof　　　☐ Floor

　　☐ Door　　　☐ Window　　☐ Windshield

3. WHEN DOES IT HAPPEN?

☐ When engine is being started　　☐ When engine is cold

☐ When engine is warming up　　☐ When engine is warmed up

☐ When engine is hot　　　　　　☐ Happens all the time

☐ After having driven for_____miles (kilometers)

☐ After having driven for___ minutes

☐ Changes with engine speed

☐ Changes with vehicle speed

☐ Only occurs when the vehicle is stopped

☐ Only occurs when accelerating

☐ Only occurs when decelerating

☐ When braking

☐ When cornering

☐ Intermittent—comes and goes with no obvious pattern

☐ At _____ mph (km/h)

☐ At any speed

☐ When using the clutch

☐ When in _____ gear

☐ When shifting from ___ gear into ___ gear

Before you sign the repair order, go over it point by point and ask questions about any item you don't understand.

❖

many of the symptoms listed, there are 20 or 30 additional possible causes that are not included.

Don't Sign the Repair Order Yet

1. Talk things over before you act. Ask questions about the repair order before you sign it. Don't be afraid to say, "I don't understand what you mean by that."

2. Read the repair order carefully before you sign it. Make certain it describes your car's trouble symptoms *specifically*. For example, the words "check engine performance" are too vague. They could mean anything. The repair order should *specifically* indicate the nature of the car's trouble symptoms—for example, "check for hesitation during first two minutes of engine warmup." It may also include the time of day, the speed, whether you're decelerating or accelerating, and how far you've traveled.

3. Ask for your old parts back (in a plastic bag for cleanliness, of course), but do so in advance. Remember

that in asking to see the old part, you could actually be shown someone else's old part, but at least you'll be making it more awkward for a dishonest person to rip you off.

4. Get a written estimate. A repair order authorizes the service facility to perform the maintenance or repairs listed on it. When you sign a work order, you agree to be responsible for the charges listed on it. Ask questions about the work before you sign. And don't be afraid to take up some of their time. Service is their business.

Estimates, Guesstimates, and Second Opinions

If there are unknowns, get a written estimate. Many states have laws that require written estimates, at least for more expensive repairs. Other laws may also require shops to get your consent to exceed the estimate, return replaced parts, provide written invoices itemizing parts and labor, and more. Check with the attorney general's office for your state's requirements. You can't beat a written estimate for security.

NAME MARY NELSON			CUST. NO. 19252		R.O. DATE 7/23/95	MILEAGE 59125	TIME REC. 8:43	TIME PROM 2:00 PM
ADDRESS 5705 S. DELEWARE DRIVE			ADVISOR 1361	RESIDENCE PHONE 303·6654	BUSINESS PHONE 345·6843			
CITY, STATE SANTA FE, NM			ZIP 87501	V/E # 747564	DEL. DATE 10/21/84	DEL. MILEAGE 1		
YR 94	MAKE CHEV.	MODEL CAVA WGN	COLOR BRN	LICENSE *&%BV	VEHICLE ID 1G1AD35P2G727315			
LABOR RATE IS BASED ON AN AVERAGE OF $65.00 PER FLAT RATE HOUR ESTIMATE OF NEEDS REPAIRS								
QUANTITY	PART NO.		PRICE	EXTENSION		EMP. NO.	COST	
	Pickup Coil		$95.	/1978503				
	Modules		$160.	/1979107				
1.5	Labor		$97.50				97.50	
	Plug Wires		$60.					
	Plugs		$20.				65.00	
1.0	Labor		$65.					
	Air Filter		$18					
	EGR Valve		$66.					
.5	Labor		$32.50				32.50	
	TOTALS					TOTALS	614.00	

Get a written estimate.

Most shops will quote a flat-rate price for your work. Using a manual that averages the time it takes for each job, they will quote and charge you a set price rather than the clock rate or actual time it takes the mechanic to perform that procedure at a given hourly rate. If you have any questions about the flat-rate price, ask to see the manual. If the price differs from that in the manual, you have a right to know why. Just as the best waiter can make a mistake in a bill, so can the best service writer or mechanic. Why not double check as you would for any other bill?

"Take it Out and Tell You Later"

If a shop refuses and says they can't give you any kind of estimate until they pull the engine or transmission apart, consider taking your car elsewhere. (This strategy of "take it out and tell you later" may even be against the law in your state.) They may not be able to tell you what is wrong with the system until it is opened up; nevertheless, at a minimum, get an estimate in writing on the cost to disassemble, diagnose, and reassemble. Always find out what the maximum charge to you could be. Remember, you can always have the car towed to another shop. Never let yourself be intimidated or pressured into a repair job you feel uncertain about. Get a second opinion, even if it means the additional cost of a tow.

If the estimate is to be exceeded by a certain amount or percentage (10 percent is a good rule of thumb), make sure you both agree that you must be notified and give your approval before the work is done. Leave a telephone number where you can be contacted and be there! Or agree on a time that you will call the mechanic to find out how things are going.

A Second Opinion

If you believe the estimate is high, are suspicious of the need for the repair, or simply want to compare prices, a second opinion makes sense. Yes, it's inconvenient and it's going to cost more money; however, the savings of hundreds of dollars or more may make it worthwhile if the original diagnosis was inaccurate or unreasonable.

It isn't always necessary to take the car to another shop, although you may want to, especially if the car is still driveable. Instead, you may be able to get a second opinion or compare a price over the telephone. First, talk to the shop and make sure you are quite clear about what the problem is, exactly what needs to be done to fix it, and how much it will cost. Write down all the information. Second, call another shop and ask what they charge to do the same repair. Be sure to give them the make, model, and year of your car first.

How to Pick Up Your Car after It Has Been Repaired

First, call the repair shop to make sure the car is ready. Allow yourself 20 minutes or more when you pick up your newly repaired car. You will need at least this much time to go over the bill and test drive the car. If you pick up your car one minute before the shop closes and then discover en route home that the problem you just paid for is still not fixed, you could find yourself talking to someone the next day who insists that the problem is a new one and intends to charge you accordingly. So arrive early whenever possible.

After you pick up your car from the shop, test drive it immediately.

The bill should be legible and understandable. A bill that is covered with smudged fingerprints and parts numbers without descriptions is not acceptable. Go over each item on the bill. If possible, speak to the person with you dealt with when you brought the car in for service. A good service provider should be willing to take the extra 10 or 15 minutes to explain, in plain English, the nature of the problem, what repairs were made, and how these steps related to your car's symptoms.

Listen to the explanations and if you don't understand them, be specific about exactly what it is you do not understand. There are no stupid questions. Ask to be shown (or drawn) a picture if words are failing. Keep asking until you are comfortable with your level of understanding. If you are satisfied with the work, let your service provider know it.

Test drive your car immediately. If you are not completely satisfied that the problem has been corrected, take your car back to the shop immediately.

What to Do If the Car Is Not Fixed Right the First, Second, or Even Third Time

Be assertive, not aggressive. Be firm, clear, and be specific about what is not right. Remember, you don't have to be disagreeable to disagree.

Request that the manager or shop foreman road test the vehicle with you in it to demonstrate that the problem has not been fixed correctly.

Give them a chance to correct the error or oversight; honest mistakes do happen. If the problem is not corrected to your satisfaction, you may need to take the following measures.

Keep Accurate Records

Keep accurate records, including all receipts and records. Include each service visit and an itemized list of what happened. Whenever possible, get a copy of the actual test results. Make certain the information includes any parts replaced and cost of labor, as well as what was said and who said it. Be sure you get the full name and title of the person with whom you speak. Date every piece of pertinent material, including each repair record. Do the same with every phone call.

Notify newspapers, radio and television consumer advocates, and private consumer groups of your problem. Be certain you send a copy of your letter to the repair shop.

LUBE, OIL AND FILTER CHANGES	DATE	MILEAGE/KILOMETERS	NOTES	OIL TYPE AND BRAND

AIR FILTER CHANGE	DATE	MILEAGE/KILOMETERS	NOTES

FUEL FILTER CHANGES	DATE	MILEAGE/KILOMETERS	NOTES

TIRE ROTATION	DATE	MILEAGE/KILOMETERS	NOTES

COOLING SYSTEM FLUSH AND REFILL	DATE	MILEAGE/KILOMETERS	NOTES

AUTOMATIC TRANSMISSION FLUID CHANGE AND FILTER	DATE	MILEAGE/KILOMETERS	NOTES

OTHER MAINTENANCE AND REPAIRS	DATE	MILEAGE/KILOMETERS	TYPE OF REPAIR OR MAINTENANCE	NOTES

Keep an up-to-date maintenance record and familiarize yourself with it before you have your car repaired.

Airing Your Complaints

Send the Better Business Bureau a copy of a letter stating the problem. Contact the Consumer Protection Agency (often a division of the attorney general's office). Ask them to refer you to any local complaint handling panels. Get as much information as possible about how the panel works, what kind of problems they handle, who handles them, how they are handled (whether by written or oral arguments), within what period of time they make their decisions, and whether they are binding on you and/or the other party.

If you are not satisfied with the results of the complaint panel, you may wish to take your claim to small claims court. You will not need a lawyer, but be certain your claim falls within the limits of the court.

If Your Car Is Under Warranty

There are many creative ways to voice dissatisfaction over repair service.

Ask the dealership whether there are any technical service bulletins related to this problem. These TSBs are special information "communiqués" that describe fixes for unusual trouble areas. The manufacturer releases these to their dealerships. They can relate to anything from brakes to body work. If there are no TSBs issued for this particular problem, the technician should call the Technical Support Center for that manufacturer to advise. These folks specialize in the hard to fix areas and often have information that even the dealership does not.

If a dealer tells you that your problem is a factory defect but there is no cure yet, be sure you get them to put it in writing.

If you are told "they all do that," ask for a demonstration test-drive in a similar vehicle.

Contact the manufacturer's customer service representative. The telephone number is usually found in your owner's manual. If you are still not satisfied, call or write the manufacturer's district or zone representative. (The name and telephone number may also be listed in your owner's manual. If not, ask the manufacturer's customer service representative for their number.) Document the details of the problem and ask the representative to meet with you to discuss them.

If you do not get a satisfactory response, pay for the cost of a written diagnosis from an independent mechanic. Do not, however, have the work done if the car is still under warranty.

Bringing in a Neutral Third Party

If you are still unsatisfied, take your case to the arbitration program of which your car manufacturer is a member. Arbitration programs are forums within which both the consumer and the dealer/manufacturer have an opportunity to state their side of the disagreement. These may be industry-run or state-run; the latter may require a filing fee. Depending on the car's warranty documentation, there may or may not be a choice as to which one to use. The jurisdiction of arbitration programs vary.

Check your warranty documents for details. If you must go to arbitration, get all the advice and information available by contacting the consumer affairs office of the state attorney general's office: how the procedure is conducted, who is on the panel, how the case is heard (whether by written or oral arguments), how long before a decision must be rendered, and if you must accept the findings of the panel. Usually decisions are binding for the manufacturer, but not for the consumer. The most important part of these proceedings is that you follow the rules of the arbitration board to the letter and that your case is well documented.

Most states have passed lemon laws.

Lemon Laws

To protect consumers from manufacturer's defects in new vehicles, most states have passed lemon laws. These laws cover problems that are so serious they result in the loss or reduction of the vehicle's use, value, and/or

Arbitration and Dispute Resolution Offices

Chrysler Customer Arbitration Board
Consult owner information packet or call Chrysler
Customer Center: (800) 992-1997

Ford Dispute Settlement Board
P.O. Box 5120
Southfield, MI 48086
(800) 241-8450

AUTOCAP
National Automotive Dealers Association
8400 Westpark Drive
McLean, VA 22102
(800) 254-NADA
Participating manufacturers: Acura, BMW, Fiat,
Honda, Isuzu, Jaguar, Mitsubishi, Nissan, Rolls-
Royce, Saab, Volvo.

BBB AUTO LINE
Better Business Bureau
(800) 955-5100
Participating manufacturers (national): Acura,
Alfa-Romeo, Audi, General Motors, Honda,
Infiniti, Isuzu, Nissan, Saturn, Volkswagen. (BMW,
Jaguar, Maserati, Mitsubishi, Peugeot, Land Rover,
Rolls-Royce, Saab, Sterling, Subaru, and Volvo also
participate in certain states.)

safety. Further, they prescribe methods for compensation
of the cost of repairs and related expenses, and in some
cases, they even recommend the replacement of the vehicle or the refund of its value.

The specific requirements for asserting your rights
under the lemon laws vary from state to state. The

coverage time may be as brief as one year or as long as two years from the date of ownership or warranty period. An authorized facility must have unsuccessfully attempted to make repairs for the same or different problem (this depends on how the state law is written) a predetermined number of times, or the car must be out of service and in the shop for a specific number of days during the coverage time. The dealer or manufacturer must be correctly notified of the problem and given the opportunity to fix it. This may mean a certified return receipt letter to the dealer, the manufacturer's customer relations office, and the local district or zone representative. Arbitration is the standard forum for resolution. If you believe your vehicle qualifies under your state's lemon law, contact your state attorney general's office and get all information related to filing a complaint. However, it is not necessary for your state to have a lemon law for you to participate in arbitration.

If your problem is safety related, call the National Highway Safety Administration's toll-free number, (800) 424-9393. They can give you information about safety standards, regulations, recalls, and references to other governmental agencies that can assist you in problem solving.

A Summary of Tips on Avoiding Car Repair Rip-Off

✔ Ask neighbors, friends, and family members to recommend reputable repair shops.

✔ Check out the repair shop before you leave your car there. How long has the company been in business? Ask about training, certification, warranties offered, and the kind of equipment they use.

✔ Keep a maintenance log of all service work done on your car.

✔ Get a written estimate and read the repair order. Make sure you understand all of it.

✓ Don't expect perfection. Even the best technicians sometimes make mistakes.

✓ If you are dissatisfied with your service and can't get satisfaction, write a letter to the company manager or president.

✓ Consider legal action as a last resort. Many repair shops will agree to resolve disputes through mediation or arbitration.

15
Safety On and Off the Road

Traveling today's highways puts everyone at greater risk as a result of the higher frequency of auto-related violence. In this chapter, you'll learn the simple precautions you can take to better protect yourself both on and off the road, including how to change a flat tire safely and easily, how to jump-start a disabled vehicle correctly, and numerous tips for traveling alone. ❖

Safety advances can be classified into two categories: protection and avoidance.

Crash protection features include seat belts, air bags, and redesign of vehicle structures. Crash avoidance features include electronically controlled brakes (ABS), traction control, better suspension designs, and better tires.

Safety has come a long way in recent years. Redesigned vehicle structures, the widespread use of seat belts, airbags, anti-lock brakes, and traction control are helping vehicles to grip even slippery roads. Collapsible steering columns and shatterproof safety glass have all contributed to protecting occupants in an accident. But protection is only part of the effort. Breakthroughs in crash avoidance technology are also taking place. In the not-too-distant future, sophisticated radar that can detect obstacles that are too close for comfort—or rather for safety—will actually enhance a driver's senses. Onboard navigation systems that tell us where we are and how to get where we want to go will help to keep us from being distracted and getting lost, and are already in use on some vehicles.

SENSORS IGNITE SODIUM AZIDE, WHICH RELEASES NITROGEN GAS.

NITROGEN DEPLOYS THE AIR BAG WITHIN 1/25 OF A SECOND AFTER IMPACT.

How air bags work

❖

Despite these advances, however, driving remains one of the more dangerous activities we engage in. Our stress levels have risen due to overcrowded highways. And at night, the stress is compounded by our awareness that our personal safety if often at risk. That risk has been heightened as the level and frequency of auto-related violence has increased. Unfortunately, our educational system is not doing an adequate job of teaching us how to respond appropriately to our changing environment. Common sense and preparation can help us to meet this challenge.

If you drive alone, you can increase your safety by taking a few simple precautions, such as parking under a streetlight at night.

Keeping your car well maintained, your gas tank at least a quarter full, and your tires properly inflated are essential ingredients of being prepared. *Note:* Being suspicious of coincidence and aware of your surroundings are additional critical success factors. But even if you conscientiously follow these general guidelines, you may have to deal with an emergency situation. If you drive alone, you can improve your personal safety by taking a few simple precautions.

Safety Precautions

Consider purchasing a cellular telephone and membership in an auto club or 24-hour towing assistance program. On many newer cars, these assistance programs are free for a limited period of time.

> ➤ Never leave your car running.
> ➤ Never leave your keys in the car.
> ➤ Never leave your car unlocked.
> ➤ Always lock yourself in the car. (Power door locks are an excellent safety feature.)

➤ When you drive into a parking lot, notice the other cars, especially if they are occupied.

➤ Always park in a well-lighted central spot, preferably one where there are frequent passersby.

➤ Whenever you leave your vehicle, push the driver's seat forward. As you approach your vehicle to re-enter, check the seat. If it is no longer pushed forward, do not enter the car. Return to a safe building and call for help.

➤ When returning to your car, keep your keys in your hand with the sharp ends protruding between your fingers. They make a good weapon.

➤ As you drive away, notice the behavior of other cars.

➤ If you suspect you are being followed, go to a public place and request that the manager call the police.

If you suspect you are being followed, go to a public place and request that the manager call the police.

❖

➤ When stopped at a stoplight, leave enough room between you and the car in front of you to be able to maneuver around it if trouble does develop.

➤ Never pick up hitchhikers. If you must for any reason talk to a stranger while you are in your vehicle, lower the window only the inch or so required to be heard.

➤ If you see someone in distress on the highway, drive to the nearest police or service station and report their plight to someone who can help them.

If your vehicle is hit from behind by another car at a stoplight or sign, do not get out of the car.

➤ If your vehicle is hit from behind, roll the window down only enough to be heard, and request the driver to follow you to the nearest police station or public place.

➤ As you drive, get in the habit of making mental notes of route numbers, locations of service stations, emergency telephones, and police stations.

➤ If you are harassed in any way, do not respond. Appear to be uninterested—not disdainful. Most of these people are looking for a reaction. If they continue to harass you, drive to a public place and have someone telephone the police.

➤ Avoid shortcuts that take you through unfamiliar or unsafe areas.

➤ If you have a garage, consider having an automatic garage door opener installed. When using an automatic garage door opener, remain in the car until the garage door has closed behind you.

➤ Consider investing your time and money in one of the top driving schools. Check the automobile magazines for names and addresses.

Warning! There is no one set of correct rules for appropriately dealing with every emergency situation. Your response will have to be conditioned by your knowledge of the area, the weather, the general safety of the road, and many other variables. As in any emergency situation, you will need to use your common sense. There is only one rule that always applies: your safety and that of your passengers comes first. Whatever it takes.

Dealing with the Dreaded Flat Tire

You're driving down the road, it's late, it's night, and you hear a loud *pop*. The car swerves violently. You take your foot off the accelerator and with firm, steady, but relaxed arms, you pick a safe spot on the side of the road and ease the car over to it.

Right now a cellular phone and the 800 number for a 24-hour towing service would look like the best investment you'd ever made, but failing that, here is what you can do to get back on the road. The first thing you do upon stopping is put the emergency flashers on and set the parking brake with the car turned off and in park or first gear. After exiting the car by the door away from the road, you pull out your fully equipped emergency kit. In it is a good flashlight with batteries that work! You take the piece

First, pull off the road with your emergency flashers on.

❖

of fluorescent material—vest, ribbon, anything you can drape over your body—and put it on so you show up in the dark. (Flat tires only happen when you're in your best dark-colored outfit.) Now take one of the two flares from the emergency kit, or the plastic reflective triangle.

You walk backward six to ten car lengths and position the triangle or flare so that it can be easily seen by oncoming traffic. If you are using flares, light the first of the two flares as you would a big match. First take the top plastic cover off. You'll find a striking surface underneath. Now remove the second, larger, plastic cover under which you will find another striking surface. Hold the flare away from your face and briskly rub striking surface against striking surface. The flare may spit sparks at you, so keep it away from your clothing as you stick it in the ground or lay it on its side. Most flares will burn for only 15 minutes. That's why you have two.

Remove the instructions for the use of your **jack** from the glove box or wherever they are located. It will help if you have practiced the following procedure prior to this occurrence in the warmth and comfort of your own well-lighted driveway or garage with several of your closest friends for company. It will also help if you purchased a 4-way (star) lug wrench that day last spring at a local auto parts or retail store. You will have had two choices when you bought yours: one is for domestic vehicles (SAE) and one is for imported vehicles (metric). (What? You don't have one? Get thee to a parts store. Tell the service personnel the make of your vehicle you are driving, and they will guide you to the best choice.)

With practice, you can change a flat tire in about 10 minutes. Helpful hint: practice in your driveway, not on a moonlit freeway.

Your emergency kit should include a first aid kit, flares or a reflective triangle, plastic chock, a flashlight and spare batteries, jumper cables, a distress flag or cloth, and a sign or auto-shade that reads, "Help, Call Police."

Ready? Good. Here's what you do:

1. Remove all the required paraphernalia: jack, lug wrench, special spare tire, plastic chock (block), and garden gloves (optional).

2. Place the chock behind the wheel that is diagonally opposite (kitty-corner to) the one that is flat. This is to ensure that even if the car does slip off the jack, it won't roll.

3. Remove the wheel covering using the method and device shown in your manual; keep it handy. If your vehicle has aluminum wheels, you will need to use the special aluminum wheel lock located in a plastic bag in the glove box, owner's manual pouch, or with the spare tire.

Changing a tire, in ten easy steps

4. Position the jack as your manual indicates, but do not raise the car with it yet.

5. First, break the tension on the lug nuts, *but don't remove them.* Since they have undoubtedly been put on with an air tool, which has the strength of eight giant weightlifters, you will need to use a length of pipe or the special star wrench to increase your leverage. The end of the wrench should fit snugly onto the lug nuts. Remember, "right is tight." Loosen the lug nuts by turning them to the left, or counter-clockwise. The only exception, and this is rare, is if the lug nuts are labeled with an "L." If they are, you will need to loosen them in the opposite direction.

Changing a tire, continued

6. Now, *slowly* engage the jack, standing slightly to one side in case the jack decides to let go. Raise the car only as high as necessary to remove the old tire and to put the new one on. You can always raise it another notch if it's too low to the ground, but the higher it goes, the less stable it is.

7. Remove the lug nuts the rest of the way by hand and put then inside the hub cap. If you miss this step and you accidentally kick one into the dirt, you can bet trying to find it in the dark will be less than amusing.

8. Roll the spare into place. Take the damaged tire off. Be particularly careful not to touch the rubber until you're sure it's cool. Blowouts increase internal tire temperatures to tropical levels, and they may remain hot for quite a while. This is why we recommend having a pair of garden gloves.

9. Put the spare on. Hand-tighten the lug nuts in a *crisscross* pattern until each one starts to make the wheel spin. Then go back and check each one again.

10. Slowly lower the jack. Take the lug wrench and tighten each one of the lugs with as much force as you can muster. As long as the lug wrench is at a right angle to the wheel, you shouldn't do any damage. Right is tight (with the above-mentioned exception).

As soon as you stow the equipment back where it came from, you can be on your way. Drive to a service station and have the original tire repaired. If the spare is a full-sized spare that can be rotated into your regular tires and is designed for doing so, you can continue to drive on it, but have the tension on the lug nuts checked by a professional as soon as possible.

If there is no safe place to pull off the road—let's say you're stuck on a narrow bridge—you will have to continue to drive the car at a reduced speed with the emergency flashers on until you reach a safe spot to pull off the road. That means the tire will probably get damaged and possibly the wheel as well—but a ruined tire is a small price to pay for your safety.

If, for whatever reason, you do not feel comfortable with the above procedure or if your vehicle has quit for a reason other than a flat tire, consider using Plan B.

Plan B: Use your emergency flashers to alert other drivers that your vehicle is disabled. Take the fluorescent sign that is also in your emergency kit—the one that says "Help, Please Call Police"—and place it in the rear window so that the traffic going in your direction can easily see it, lock your door, and open it only for a uniformed policeman or legitimate tow truck representative. If someone else stops to help you, the safest thing you can do under most circumstances is to remain in the car and speak with them only through an inch or so of rolled-down window (enough for you to be heard). Thank them for their offer of help and ask them to call the police and tow truck.

How to jump-start a battery

Jump-Starting a Battery

Keeping up with routine maintenance will hopefully keep you from ever having to jump-start your car, but you should know the procedure, in case an emergency presents itself.

Move the two cars close, *but do not allow them to touch.* Turn off the ignition and all electrical accessories except for the emergency flashers if needed.

All batteries and jumper cables are color coded. Red is positive. Black is negative. Here's how to jump-start a battery:

1. Connect the red jumper cable first to the dead battery's positive terminal.

2. Connect the other end of the red jumper cable to the positive terminal of the helper battery.

3. Connect the black jumper cable to the negative terminal of the helper battery.

4. Connect the other end of the black jumper cable to an unpainted piece of metal (a bolt is a good choice) on the stalled engine.

5. Start the helper car, then the stalled car.

6. Remove jumper cables in the exact *opposite order.*

Warning!

Do not attempt to jump-start or recharge a battery when the indicator is clear. It generally means the battery is low on water, and high on hydrogen gas. A spark could cause an explosion.

Electrical Fire

If you notice a fire under the hood—and, if one were burning, chances are you would—drive the car to a safe area, stop, pull the inside hood latch, and get yourself and your passengers out of the car and to safety immediately. Go to the nearest phone and call the fire department. Do *not* open the hood of the car. The extra oxygen that is added by opening the hood may feed the fire. You have already helped by releasing the hood's interior latch. Stay away from the car while you are awaiting the arrival of the fire department and let professionals put the fire out.

Glossary

Afterfire—the tendency of an engine to continue to burn the air/fuel mixture after the engine has been turned off. Also called dieseling or engine run-on.

Air conditioning condenser—a device that cools refrigerant, causing it to give up heat.

Air filter—a filter, made of pleated folds of paper, designed to catch dust and dirt.

Alignment—*see* Wheel alignment

Alternator—a motor that produces electric current.

Amperes (amps)— a measurement of electricity's strength or intensity.

Analog—a system for representing information based on the numerical system.

Antenna—a device that sends out or receives radio waves.

Antifreeze—a substance, usually ethylene glycol, added to a car's water cooling system to keep it from freezing in winter and boiling over in summer.

Anti-lock brakes—electronically controlled brakes that help the driver maintain control and prevent wheel lock-up during hard braking.

Arc—the discharge of an electric current across a gap.

Automatic transmission—a transmission in which the gears are shifted automatically by the engine's torque converter.

Axle—the rod or shaft on which a wheel turns.

Backfire—an explosion of the air/fuel mixture that exits the engine or exhaust.

Balance shaft—a shaft that uses weights to spread out the vibrations produced by an engine.

Ball joint—a coupling device that permits movement between parts.

Battery—a device that stores and generates electricity.

Beads—thin strips of metal wound together into a narrow ring that provides a tire with an airtight grip on the wheel.

Bearing—a device that distributes and supports weight while reducing friction.

BHP—an abbreviation for brake horsepower: the amount of power an engine delivers after taking into account the forces of friction, including inertia and wind resistance.

Bias-belted tire—a tire that is constructed in such a way that the plies meet each other on the diagonal and are reinforced with strips of metal or fiberglass.

Bias-ply tire—a tire that is constructed in such a way that the materials meet each other on the diagonal.

Bonding—a gluing process.

Boot—a rubber device that covers and protects a coupler or connecting point.

Brake fade—*see* Fading

Brake lights—the lights located at the rear of a vehicle that warn following vehicles that the driver is braking.

Brake lines—lines that carry brake fluid from the master cylinder to the brakes at each wheel.

Brake lining—heat-resistant material that lines the moving parts (shoes) of drum brakes.

Brake shoe—a crescent-shaped piece of metal that is lined with heat-resistant materials.

Break in—the period of time in a new vehicle's life before it attains top efficiency. It may require special precautionary measures to be taken by the driver.

Bumper—a steel or metal bar located at the front or rear of a vehicle that helps to prevent or limit damage to the vehicle in a minor collision.

Bumper-to-bumper warranty—the manufacturer's guarantee that everything in a vehicle, from the front bumper to the rear bumper, except for normal wear and tear items and those items that are specifically excluded, will be free of defects and perform in a specific way.

Bushing—a metal or rubber liner that reduces wear between two metal parts by acting as a cushion.

Caliper—the brake component that works like a fist, with one or two fingers (pistons) that force disc brake pads against the rotor, causing it to slow or stop the vehicle.

Camshaft—a bar or shaft with metal bumps or lobes (called cams) that regulates the opening and closing of the engine's valves. Engines are often classified by the number and position of the camshaft(s) within the engine, i.e., single (SOHC) or dual (DOHC) overhead cam engine.

Capacitor—*see* Condenser

Carbon deposits—the natural accumulation of the byproducts of combustion within the engine. Over time these deposits can adversely affect engine performance.

Carburetor—a device that combines air and fuel and distributes this mixture to the cylinders.

Catalytic converter—an emission control component containing exotic metals and chemically treated substances that turn pollutants into such harmless substances as water and carbon dioxide.

Cell—a device that produces electric current. Most batteries have six cells that are connected together. Also a unit of memory in a computer that stores information.

Chassis—the steel frame or platform of an automobile. Chassis are still found on most trucks but have been replaced in most modern passenger vehicles by a unibody construction.

Choke—a door or plate located on top of the carburetor that closes when it is cold, forcing more gasoline into the air/fuel mixture.

Circuit—a source of current and a series of devices that allow current to flow through them to electrical components.

Clutch—a device that connects and disconnects the wheels from the engine.

Clutch disc—a plate, covered with friction material, that is squeezed against the flywheel when the clutch pedal is released.

Coil—a booster or magnifier of electrical current.

Coil spring—a suspension component that compresses and extends in response to irregularities in the road surface.

Combustion—the burning of the air/fuel mixture.

Combustion chamber—the upper area within the cylinders where the air/fuel mixture is burned.

Compression—the squeezing or compressing of the air/fuel mixture into a fraction of its former space.

Compression ratio—a numerical comparison: the size of a cylinder when the piston is at its lowest point of travel compared with the size of the cylinder when the piston is at its highest point of travel; expressed in a ratio such as 12:1.

Compression stroke—the second movement of a piston in a four-stroke engine, which compresses the fuel mixture into a small space at the top of the combustion chamber.

Compressor—a machine that compresses gas.

Computer—*see* Engine control module

Condenser—a tiny sponge that absorbs excess current.

Conductor—any material that offers little or no resistance to the flow of electricity.

Connecting rod—the metal piece that connects the piston to the crankshaft.

Constant velocity joint (CV joint)—the coupler where the driving and driven shafts meet on a front-wheel drive vehicle.

Control arms—the metal arms that attach the wheels to the frame of a car.

Coolant—a solution of water and ethylene glycol that draws heat away from the engine.

Coolant reservoir—a translucent container that serves as an overflow for expanding coolant.

Cooling system—the components that help to keep an engine from overheating. These include but are not limited to the radiator, radiator cap, thermostat, and water pump.

Coupe—a sports car design.

Crankcase—the metal casing surrounding the crankshaft.

Crankshaft—the bar to which the pistons are attached. The crankshaft converts the up-and-down motion of the pistons into rotational motion.

Crankshaft balancer—a weighted object that is attached to a crankshaft to smooth out the vibrations of the engine. It is also called a harmonic balancer.

Current—the flow of electrical charge.

Cutting—shaving off a thin layer of metal from the brake rotors or drums to remove surface irregularities. Also known as turning.

Cylinder—a hollow tube cut into the engine block that houses the pistons.

Cylinder head—the portion of the engine casing in which the valves are located.

Data—information that a computer stores and uses to perform a task.

Detonation—an irregular burning of the air/fuel mixture.

Diesel engine—an engine in which the spark is ignited by heat alone.

Differential—a specialized transmission that allows a car's outside wheels to travel farther and faster than the inside wheels while cornering.

Digital—a computerized system with numerical readouts, based on the binary system.

Dimmer switch—the switch that dims the headlights of a vehicle.

Dipstick—a rod used for measuring the volume of fluids.

Disc brake—a type of brake that uses a caliper and kidney-shaped brake pad lined with heat-resistant material to stop a car.

Distributor—the ignition component that distributes voltage to the spark plugs.

Distributor cap—the plastic cap that covers the distributor.

Distributorless ignition—a modern ignition system in which the computer performs the tasks of the distributor.

Double overhead cam engine (DOHC)—a common modern engine layout for a multi-valve engine in which the two camshafts that open and close the valves are located near the top of the engine.

Drag—air or water resistance that tends to slow down a moving object.

Drain plug—the plug through which oil is drained from an engine.

Driveability—a term that refers to a variety of performance problems that cannot be readily diagnosed or easily fixed.

Driveshaft—the bar that connects the transmission output shaft to the rear axles in a rear wheel drive vehicle.

Drum brakes—a type of brake that uses a metal canister and two crescent-shaped brake shoes/linings to stop a car.

Dry gas—an alcohol additive that helps prevent gas line freeze-up.

Electrolyte—a solution of water and sulfuric acid that when activated causes the opposite charges of the different plate metals to react chemically.

Electronic ignition—a modern ignition system in which the components are computerized.

Emission controls—devices that reduce pollutants or chemically change them into harmless substances.

Energy—the ability to do work.

Engine analyzer—a testing device used to diagnose engine performance problems.

Engine block—the lower part of the engine, in which the pistons and cylinders are located.

Engine control module (ECM)—the heart of the computer; this component interprets instructions and causes them to be executed. Also called an engine control unit (ECU).

Engine head—a separate metal casing, placed over the engine block, that holds most of a car's valve train components.

Ethanol gasoline—a grain-based, specially formulated oxygenated gasoline that helps reduce pollutants.

Evaporative emission control system—a system that traps fuel vapors and redirects them to the engine, where they are stored until the engine starts and then burned.

Exhaust gas conversion system—an emission control system consisting of the catalytic converter and oxygen sensor.

Exhaust gas emissions analyzer—an emissions testing device that can be used to determine internal engine damage by detecting the presence of exhaust gases in the radiator.

Exhaust gas recirculation system—a system that redirects exhaust gases back to the intake manifold, where they are burned again.

Exhaust manifold—a set of cast iron pipes attached to the engine that route burned gases away from the engine.

Exhaust stroke—the fourth movement of the pistons in a four-stroke engine, which opens an exhaust value to expel hot used gases.

Exhaust system—a series of metal components that are welded together to route burned gases away from the engine and into the atmosphere.

Exhaust valve—a valve (or one-way door) opening to permit burned gases to exit an engine's combustion cylinder after each burning.

Expansion valve—the valve (or one-way door) in the air conditioning system that regulates flow of refrigerant into the evaporator.

Evaporator—an air conditioning component, consisting of a series of coils, that turns a liquid into vapor and absorbs heat.

Fading—loss of effectiveness as a result of heavy use such as with brakes.

Fan belt—a belt that transfers power from the engine and drives the engine cooling fan.

Feed-back carburetor—carburetor assisted by an external computer.

Firing order—the sequence in which spark plugs fire.

Fittings—places where metal parts are joined together.

Flashing unit—a switch that controls the directional signal lightbults, turning them on and off from 60 to 120 times a minue.

Flywheel—a large, heavy disk that is attached to and turns the camshaft.

Four-wheel drive—a power train that transfers power to all four wheels.

Four-wheel steering—a system in which both the rear wheels and the front wheels steer.

Friction—the rubbing of a surface of one object against another.

Front-wheel drive—a power train that transfers power to the car's front wheels.

Fuel filler cap—part of the evaporative emission control system.

Fuel filter—the filter that is responsible for cleaning gasoline by catching dirt and foreign particles before they reach the working parts of the carburetor or fuel injectors.

Fuel injection—a computerized method of supplying fuel to an engine by injecting fuel into the cylinders. It is the modernized equivalent of a carburetor.

Fuel injector—the device that squirts the fuel into the engine in a fuel injection system.

Fuel lines—lines that carry fuel from the fuel tank of the car to the engine.

Fuel pump—the mechanism that draws fuel from the fuel

tank to the engine. It may be mechanically or electrically powered.

Fuel sock—a coarse filter located in the fuel tank.

Fuse—the thin wire encased in plastic or glass that guards the electrical system by melting in response to surges of excess electricity.

Fusible link—a light piece of wire placed in a circuit which melts in response to surges of electricity. Similar to a fuse but without a protective casing.

Gasket—a flat piece of material that acts as a seal between two surfaces that are joined together.

Gas line freeze-up—refers to the formation of ice crystals in gasoline during cold weather, which starves the engine of fuel by clogging fuel lines.

Gasoline engine—a device that uses internal combustion (burns fuel) to produce power.

Gas-powered shock absorber—a highly efficient shock absorber that uses a nitrogen charge to pressurize the fluid in the tubes.

Gear ratio—the number of turns a driving gear makes compared to the number made by driven gear.

Gears—metal-toothed wheel sets used to transmit turning power.

Glazing—a hard, ice-like substance that forms on belts, clutch discs, and brake pads and resists melting. Glazing reduces efficiency and is often responsible for noises.

Grille—the grid on the front of an automobile.

Ground—an electrical strap or wire that completes an electrical circuit by returning it to the battery through the metal frame of he car.

Halfshaft—the right-side or left-side bar or shaft that is located between the differential and the wheels on a front-wheel drive vehicle.

Harmonic balancer—*see* Crankshaft balance

Head gasket—the gasket that seals the opening where the engine block and the engine head meet.

Headpipes—steel exhaust pipes that carry combustion gases from the manifold to the catalytic converter.

Heater control valve—a one-way door through which

coolant travels form the engine to the heater core.

Heater core—a small radiator that takes heat from hot coolant and blows the heat into the passenger compartment using an electric fan.

Hood—the bodywork of the car that covers the engine.

Horsepower—a way of measuring the power of an engine. Usually the more horsepower an engine has, the more powerful it is.

Hydraulic system—any system that operates by fluid under pressure.

Hydrometer—a device that measures the amount of sulfuric acid remaining in the battery's electrolyte solution.

Hydroplaning—a condition that causes a vehicle to lose traction when a layer of water is formed between the tires and the road surface.

Idle—the description of an engine's performance when the driver is not applying pressure to the gas pedal.

Ignition control module—a computer chip that controls the delivery of the spark to the engine.

Ignition system—the components that deliver the spark to the air/fuel mixture at the correct times.

Impeller—the portion of the torque converter that is attached to the flywheel.

Independent suspension—a suspension system in which each wheel responds independently to changes in the surface of the road.

Inertia—the tendency of moving or resting objects to continue in their moving or resting states until an external force is applied.

Input shaft—the shaft or rod leading from the engine to the transmission.

Insulator—material that offers substantial resistance to the flow of electricity.

Intake manifold—the metal tubing, bolted to the engine, through which the air/fuel mixture reaches the cylinders.

Intake port—the passageway from the intake manifold into the cylinder.

Intake stroke—the initial movement in a four stroke cycle engine, when the piston descends into the cylinder in order to allow room for the air/fuel mixture to enter.

Intake valve—the engine component that opens and closes to allow air and fuel to enter the combustion chamber.

Internal combustion—the burning of an air/fuel mixture inside an engine to produce power.

Intercooler—a device used in combination with turbochargers and superchargers that cools air and can add power.

Input shaft—the shaft leading from the engine to the transmission.

Jack—a device that is used to raise all or part of a heavy object a short distance.

Jet—an opening through which fuel passes in a carburetor.

Journal—the part of a rod or shaft that turns on a bearing.

Knocking—a heavy metallic rattling or clicking similar to marbles or ball bearings hitting together that is often related to an irregular burning of the air/fuel mixture.

Laser—a device that produces a very thin, intense beam of light waves of the same frequency.

Lateral runout—the wobble of a tire or wheel.

Leaf springs—suspension components consisting of uneven strips of metal that absorb the motion of the car's wheels as they flatten and unflatten.

Lean fuel mixture—an air/fuel mixture containing less than the normal amount of gasoline.

Lever—a rod or handle that moves to produce another movement.

Linkage—any system of rods and levers.

Load—the weight of an object that is being moved or the resistance of an object to being moved.

Load tester—a diagnostic tool that determines the health of a battery by simulating electrical load or need.

LOF—abbreviation for the maintenance procedures "lube, oil, and filter," which include lubricating a car's grease fittings and changing the engine oil and filter.

Lube job—a procedure that removes old grease and replaces it with clean grease.

Lubricant—any substance that protects an object by coating it with a thin film. Lubricants provide a slippery cushion that prevents friction.

Lubrication system—the system for pumping oil to the working parts of an engine.

MacPherson strut—a suspension component that combines the spring and shock absorber in one unit.

Manual transmission—a transmission in which the driver determines the gear selection by shifting a gear selector. Also referred to as a standard transmission.

Master cylinder—a reservoir for brake fluid that is divided into two separate sections, each section activating a different pair of brakes.

Memory—the part of the computer that stores information and instructions.

Misfire—an irregularity in the igniting of the air/fuel mixture.

Molecule—the smallest division of a compound.

Momentum—the strength or force an object gains through motion.

MTBE—one of the specially formulated oxygenated gasolines that help to reduce pollutants. It is synthetically made.

Muffler—part of the exhaust system, this device absorbs much of the sound that combustion creates by routing sound waves through its hollow chambers.

Multi-grade oil—oil containing additives that give it the qualities of more than one grade of oil.

Multi-port fuel injection—a computerized system of supplying fuel to an engine that delivers an ideal amount of fuel into each cylinder through individual fuel injectors.

Multi-valve engine—an engine that is equipped with additional intake and/or exhaust valves that permit the engine to breathe and burn more air and fuel.

Normally aspirated—an engine that draws the air/fuel mixture into the combustion chambers without assistance.

Octane—the rating of a gasoline's ability to resist pinging or knocking.

Odometer—a dashboard instrument that records the distance that an automobile travels.

Ohms—a measurement of resistance to the flow of current.

Oil—a liquid, usually petroleum based, that acts as a lubricant.

Oil filter—a pleated paper device where dirt and contaminants are caught and stored.

Oil galley—an enclosed passageway, with smaller passageways leading from it, through which oil moves to lubricate vital engine parts.

Oil pressure gauge—the dashboard instrument that registers oil pressure.

Oil pump—a pump that pressurizes oil and circulates it through the engine.

Open—any electrical wiring condition that interrupts the flow of current.

Oscilloscope—a diagnostic tool that gives a visual picture of the ignition system's activity.

Output shaft—the shaft leading from the transmission to the wheels.

Overdrive—a fuel-saving gear that can be used at highway speeds.

Overflow reservoir—the translucent tank or container that is part of the cooling system.

Overhead cam engine (OHC)—a common modern engine layout in which the camshaft is located near the top of the engine. Engines are frequently identified by where the camshaft is located.

Oversteer—the tendency of a car to turn too sharply when cornering.

Oxygen sensor—a device that monitors the richness or leanness of the fuel mixture.

Parallelogram steering—a term describing the shape of the rods and levers that enclose the steering gears in a box at the lower end of the steering column.

Parking brake—the brake that holds a vehicle motionless while it is parked.

Pinging—a light metallic rattling or clicking similar to marbles or ball bearings hitting together.

Piston—a cylindrical-shaped metal plug that moves up and down within the cylinders to compress the air/fuel mixture. It is also a device that can be used to transmit the force of liquid under pressure (hydraulics). Brake calipers and wheel cylinders have pistons for this purpose.

Piston ring—a metal hoop that surrounds the pistons and helps to seal the combustion chambers.

Planetary gears—gear sets that provide changes in gear ratios in automatic transmissions.

Plates—the interior walls of a battery. Plates absorb chemicals and with age develop hard, crusty deposits that block the passage of electrical currents.

Play—looseness or lack of responsiveness in the steering wheel.

Plies—pieces of material attached to the bead of the tire. The materials and the angle at which they meet each other determine the tire's construction category.

Points—a component of earlier ignition systems, these metal arms open and close, causing the coil to become saturated with electricity.

Port—the connecting passageway between the intake manifold and the cylinder where the valves are located.

Positive crankcase ventilation system—a system that picks up gases which have escaped into the crankcase from the combustion chambers and returns them to the engine to be burned.

Power brakes—brakes that use the power of the engine to stop the car.

Power loss—a condition causing the engine to continue to run, but at dramatically reduced speed.

Power steering—the assistance, provided by hydraulic fluid, that can be added to make steering easier.

Power stroke—the third movement of the pistons in a four stroke engine. The piston moves down into the cylinder as a result of the expansion of exploding gases.

Power train warranty—the manufacturer's guarantee that the heavier components of a vehicle, including the engine, transmission, differential, and drive axles, will be free of defects and perform in a specific way.

Preheated air intake system—the system designed to warm the air entering the engine to the correct temperature.

Pressure plate—the clutch component that squeezes the

clutch disk against the flywheel when the clutch pedal is released.

Printed circuit—a board with a printed pattern of metal connectors that conducts current to electronic components attached to the board.

PROM (programmable read-only memory)—a computer chip that permanently stores information; information on this chip cannot be changed or altered, only reviewed and read.

Prorated—a way of assessing compensation or value based on the proportion of the use of the item.

Prototype—an experimental vehicle used to test a new design.

Pushrod engine—an engine layout in which the camshaft is located lower in the engine and operates the opening and closing of the valves through a variety of additional components.

Rack and pinion—a lightweight steering system consisting of a pinion gear (one with a small number of teeth) and a long rack with teeth.

Radial runout—the difference between high and low points on a tire tread.

Radial tire—a tire with lines (cords) that develop symmetrically from a central point, like the spokes of a wheel. The construction materials meet each other at right angles and are reinforced with strips of steel.

Radiator—a device that stores and circulates coolant.

Radiator cap—the cap of a radiator that contributes to maintaining the proper pressure and temperature within the cooling system.

Rear-wheel drive—a vehicle layout where power is transmitted from the engine to only the rear wheels.

Rebuilt—a part that has been restored to a nearly new condition and resold as a replacement.

Receiver—a dryer that separates and removes moisture in the air conditioning system.

Refrigerant—a low-boiling-point fluid that absorbs heat; used in the air-conditioning system.

Relays—backup safety switches that are used on circuits where strong current develops.

Release fork—a metal arm that connects clutch components to the crankshaft.

Resonator—a sound-reducing device that diminishes noise created by combustion gases as they exit the exhaust system.

Rich fuel mixture—an air/fuel mixture containing more than the normal amount of gasoline.

Ring—*see* Piston ring

Ring gear—the outer gear in an automatic transmission. Inside it sit the sun and planetary gears.

Rocker arm—the component connecting the camshaft to the valves in a pushrod engine.

Rotor—a metal disc connected to the wheel. Also an ignition component in earlier model vehicles that directs the spark to each of the spark plugs.

Rotary engine—an engine that converts power directly into circular motion (unlike piston engines, which convert the up-and-down motion of pistons into circular motion).

Scheduled service—a list of preventive maintenance procedures that manufacturers recommend be performed at specific intervals.

Seal beam—a type of headlight in which all parts are sealed in one unit.

Sedan—a car having two or four doors and seating four or more people.

Seize—a condition that occurs within an engine when the internal components are badly damaged from too much heat and abruptly stop moving.

Selector fork—the lever that allows the driver to select a transmission gear.

Sending unit—a device that monitors volume or temperature.

Sensor—a device that receives and feeds back data.

Shock absorber—a sealed suspension component system filled with fluid that contributes to the smoothness or harshness of the ride.

Short—a circuit that is accidentally shortened, forcing the electrical current to return to its source before it reaches its destination.

Sludge—the unburned deposits that form as a result of combustion.

Solenoid—an electromagnetic object that acts as a switch.

Spark plug—a metal and ceramic device that produces a spark.

Specific gravity reading—the measurement of a battery's state of charge.

Spring—a suspension component that compresses and extends to absorb the motion of the wheels on irregular ground.

Stall—a sudden stopping of the engine.

Starter—an electrical motor that starts the engine running by turning the crankshaft.

Stator—a vaned wheel that causes fluid to swirl in one direction only.

Steering—the system of rods, levers, and gears that controls the direction of a car.

Steering gear box—a unit containing gears that take the rotational movement of the steering wheel and turn it into the side-to-side movement of the wheels.

Stroke—each movement of a piston, up or down.

Strut—a rod or bar used in the suspension system to provide structural strength.

Sump—the oil reservoir in the bottom of the engine wheel.

Sun gear—the central gear in an automatic transmission system.

Supercharger—a belt-driven device that forces an engine to produce more power by breathing more air.

Suspension—the system that controls the car's up-and-down motion.

Switch—a piece of metal suspended between two pieces of wire that serves as a gate for the electrical current, turning current off and on.

Synchronizers—toothed devices, found in manual transmissions, that synchronize the speeds of the gear combinations, preventing them from clashing.

Synthetic oil—a lubricant made in the chemist's laboratory that can reach moving parts quicker than petroleum-based oils.

Tachometer—an instrument that records the rotations of

the crankshaft and, therefore, engine speed.

Tail pipe—the final exhaust pipe, through which burned gases reach the outside air.

Tappets—levers or cams designed to touch or tap another engine component to cause movement.

Thermostat—a one-way heat-sensitive door that permits the flow of coolant to the radiator once a predetermined temperature is reached.

Throttle—a device that controls the supply of fuel.

Throttle body fuel injection—a mixing system that sprays a common measure of air/fuel to the cylinders.

Throttle position sensor—an electronic eye that relays information to the computer about the throttle opening.

Throw-out bearing—a clutch component resembling a metal doughnut that disengages the clutch.

Tie rod—in a rack and pinion steering system, rods that connect the rack to the car's wheels.

Tie rod end—the coupler in the steering system that connects the tie rods to the steering knuckle.

Timing belt (chain)—the belt linking the camshaft to the crankshaft, forcing one to turn when the other does.

Toe in—the alignment setting that refers to the rear edges of a tire being farther apart than the leading edges.

Toe out—the alignment setting that refers to the leading edges of a tire being farther apart than the rear edges.

Top dead center (TDC)—the uppermost point of a piston's travel within the cylinder.

Torque—a turning or twisting force. The torque of an engine is the maximum turning power or force produced at a specific speed.

Torque converter—the mechanism that connects and disconnects the engine from the wheels in an automatic transmission.

Torque steer—the tendency of some front-wheel drive vehicles to pull to one side upon acceleration.

Torque wrench—a specialized wrench that can be calibrated to apply a specific amount of force to a bolt.

Torsion bar—a spring that absorbs road motion by means of a bar that twists and turns.

Traction—a wheel's road grip.

Transaxle—the component that transmits the power of the

engine to the front wheels in a front-wheel drive vehicle. It combines both the transmission and the differential.

Transfer case—in four-wheel drive, a special, third set of gears that lock the front and real wheels together.

Transmission—the gear mechanism linking the power of the engine to the wheels.

Transmission fluid—a lightweight oil used in the torque converter of an automatic transmission.

Transverse engine—an engine that is positioned across a vehicle.

Tread—the grooved face of an automobile tire.

Tread depth indicator—a device that is inserted into various grooves in a tire to measure tread depth.

Trouble code—the code number, generated by an on-board computer and stored in its memory, that specifies an engine fault.

Tune-up—the routine replacement of spark plugs, filters, and other air, fuel, and ignition-related parts, plus a precise series of tests and adjustments performed at specific intervals, for the purpose of regaining maximum engine performance.

Tuning—adjusting the engine for the purpose of regaining maximum engine performance.

Turbine—a device with blades that spins fluids around.

Turbocharger—a device that adds horsepower or boost to an engine by forcing more air into the cylinders.

Two-stroke engine—an engine in which the second stroke or movement is the power stroke.

Understeer—the tendency of a vehicle to continue going straight while cornering despite the turning of the steering wheel.

Unibody—a vehicle design that uses sheet metal, rather than a separate steel frame, as part of the vehicle's platform.

Universal joint (U-joint)—the metal connecting units that facilitate movement between shafts.

Vacuum—engine-produced pressure that is lower than the outside air pressure. Also a space that has no air or gas in it.

Vacuum leak—the loss of vacuum in an engine as a result of a leaking gasket or hose, usually resulting in a performance problem.

Valve clearance—the gap that exists between the top of the valve and the part that opens and closes it. In some vehicles valve clearance is adjustable.

Valve control body—the compartment containing tiny passageways in which pressurized transmission fluid collects.

Valve guides—metal shells or sleeves within which the valves move up and down.

Valves—one-way doors located over the cylinders that regulate the flow of the air/fuel mixture into and out of the cylinders.

Valve seat—the surface a valve touches when it closes.

Valve train—components that help the valves open and close, including springs, rocker arms, pushrods, and tappets.

Vapor storage canister—a charcoal canister that holds fuel system vapors which have been redirected from the engine for reuse.

Vaporize—to convert a liquid or solid substance into a gaseous one; may create a fine mist or spray.

Vapor lock—a condition that occurs when gasoline turns from a liquid to a vapor, resulting in an engine that is starved for fuel.

Variable load shock absorber—a shock absorber that mechanically or electronically responds differently to various weights carried in the car.

Variable ratio power steering—a power steering system in which power assistance is continually monitored and electronically adjusted to levels appropriate for current driving speeds.

V-belt—the belt that transfers power from the engine to the alternator, water pump, power steering pump, and air conditioner. Also called a drive belt.

V-engine—an engine in which the cylinders are laid out in a the formation of the letter *V*.

VIN—abbreviation for a vehicle identification number, or serial number, located at the base of the windshield on a metal label.

Viscosity—refers to the measure of an oil's ability to flow at different temperatures.

Viscosity index improvers—additives that give an oil the qualities of more than one grade of oil.

Volatility—the capability of a substance such as gasoline to burn or explode easily.

Voltage—the force or pressure of electricity.

Voltage regulator—a device that regulates the flow of the alternator's current.

Warranty—the manufacturer's guarantee that a vehicle will be free of defects and perform in a specific way.

Wastegate—a device that regulates the amount of extra boost a turbocharger can deliver to an engine.

Water jacket—the sleeve of copper-lined passageways inside the engine block and head through which coolant circulates.

Water pump—a device that circulates coolant.

Wattage—the amount of power produced by an electrical current, as measured in thousands of watts or kilowatts and kilowatt-hours.

Wear bar—a patch of smooth rubber inserted into the tread of a tire that, when visible, indicates it is time to replace the tires.

Wheel alignment—the adjustment or positioning of suspension components so that the car's wheels meet the road at a specific angle.

Wheel balancing—a procedure in which small pieces of metal, called weights, are attached to the lighter spots on a wheel to make it turn evenly.

Wheelbase—the distance between the front and the rear axles.

Wheel bearing—a device that resembles a metal doughnut with many ball bearings inside that distribute the weight and turning force of a shaft.

Wheel chock—a triangular piece of wood or plastic that can be placed next to a tire to keep a vehicle from rolling.

Wheel cylinder—a device that pushes out against drum brake linings, causing the wheel to slow or stop.

Wheel-spin—the excessive movement of a wheel that results in the loss of traction.

Wind-up—the strain felt by the power train when both

axles of a standard, part-time four-wheel drive vehicle are locked together and forced to turn at the same speed on dry pavement.

Winterizing—the maintenance involved in preparing a vehicle for the winter.

Wiring harness—a group of electrical wires.

APPENDIX

TROUBLESHOOTING CHART INDEX

Following is a listing of the most common car trouble symptoms and an index to the corresponding troubleshooting chart. Identify your car's symptom and then check the troubleshooting charts on the pages listed for possible causes.

Diagnostic Toolbox

Following is some of the equipment professional technicians use to service your car. With these tools, the guesswork is taken out of diagnosis and service. Look for a technician or repair shop that utilizes these tools—or you may find yourself dealing with a "remove and replace" mechanic.

The test light and pressure gauge are used to determine problems with fuel pressure in the fuel delivery system.

The oscilloscope checks the condition of plugs, plug wires, coil, and distributor cap and rotor, much as an EEG checks for brain waves.

The compression tester can identify a leaky or bad head gasket, a bad valve, bad rings, and even a cracked cylinder head.

A pressure tester can pinpoint a leak in the cooling system.

The multimeter checks the electrical system for shorts, opens, and starting problems.

A micrometer checks the thickness of your brakes' rotors. There is a legal limit to the thickness of rotors—if yours fall below this limit, they must be replaced.

The scan tool is a device which can access the computer's trouble codes, thus identifying a multitude of problems.

INDEX

Other Books from John Muir Publications

Travel Books by Rick Steves

Asia Through the Back Door, 4th ed., 400 pp. $17.95

Europe 101: History, Art, and Culture for the Traveler, 5th ed., 368 pp. $17.95

Mona Winks: Self-Guided Tours of Europe's Top Museums, 3rd ed., 432 pp. $18.95

Rick Steves' Best of Baltics and Russia, 144 pp. $9.95

Rick Steves' Best of Europe, 544 pp. $16.95

Rick Steves' Best of France, Belgium, and the Netherlands, 240 pp. $12.95

Rick Steves' Best of Germany, Austria, and Switzerland, 240 pp. $12.95

Rick Steves' Best of Great Britain, 192 pp. $11.95

Rick Steves' Best of Italy, 208 pp. $11.95

Rick Steves' Best of Scandinavia, 192 pp. $11.95

Rick Steves' Best of Spain and Portugal, 192 pp. $11.95

Rick Steves' Europe Through the Back Door, 480 pp. $17.95

Rick Steves' French Phrase Book, 2nd ed., 176 pp. $4.95

Rick Steves' German Phrase Book, 2nd ed., 176 pp. $4.95

Rick Steves' Italian Phrase Book, 2nd ed., 176 pp. $4.95

Rick Steves' Spanish and Portuguese Phrase Book, 2nd ed., 304 pp. $5.95

Rick Steves' French/ German/Italian Phrase Book, 320 pp. $6.95

A Natural Destination Series

Belize: A Natural Destination, 3rd ed., 336 pp. $16.95

Costa Rica: A Natural Destination, 3rd ed., 400 pp. $17.95

Guatemala: A Natural Destination, 2nd ed., 352 pp. $16.95

Undiscovered Islands Series

Undiscovered Islands of the Caribbean, 4th ed., 264 pp. $16.95

Undiscovered Islands of the Mediterranean, 2nd ed., 256 pp. $13.95

Undiscovered Islands of the U.S. and Canadian West Coast, 208 pp. $12.95

For Birding Enthusiasts

The Birder's Guide to Bed and Breakfasts: U.S. and Canada, 2nd ed., 416 pp. $17.95

The Visitor's Guide to the Birds of the Central

National Parks: U.S. and Canada, 400 pp. $15.95

The Visitor's Guide to the Birds of the Eastern National Parks: U.S. and Canada, 400 pp. $15.95

The Visitor's Guide to the Birds of the Rocky Mountain National Parks: U.S. and Canada, 432 pp. $15.95

Unique Travel Series

Each is 112 pages and $10.95 paperback, except Georgia.

Unique Arizona
Unique California
Unique Colorado
Unique Florida
Unique Georgia ($11.95)
Unique New England
Unique New Mexico
Unique Texas
Unique Washington

2 to 22 Days Itinerary Planners

2 to 22 Days in the American Southwest, 192 pp. $11.95

2 to 22 Days in Asia, 192 pp. $10.95

2 to 22 Days in Australia, 192 pp. $11.95

2 to 22 Days in California, 192 pp. $11.95

2 to 22 Days in Eastern Canada, 240 pp. $12.95

2 to 22 Days in Florida, 1995 ed., 192 pp. $11.95

2 to 22 Days Around the Great Lakes, 192 pp.

9/09
10/1
11/05

$11.95

2 to 22 Days in Hawaii, 192 pp. $11.95

2 to 22 Days in New England, 192 pp. $11.95

2 to 22 Days in New Zealand, 192 pp. $11.95

2 to 22 Days in the Pacific Northwest, 192 pp. $11.95

2 to 22 Days in the Rockies, 192 pp. $11.95

2 to 22 Days in Texas, 192 pp. $11.95

2 to 22 Days in Thailand, 192 pp. $10.95

22 Days Around the World, 264 pp. $13.95

Other Terrific Travel Titles

The 100 Best Small Art Towns in America, 224 pp. $12.95

The Big Book of Adventure Travel, 2nd ed., 384 pp. $17.95

Environmental Vacations: Volunteer Projects to Save the Planet, 2nd

ed., 248 pp. $16.95

A Foreign Visitor's Survival Guide to America, 224 pp. $12.95

Great Cities of Eastern Europe, 256 pp. $16.95

Indian America: A Traveler's Companion, 4th ed., 480 pp. $18.95

Interior Furnishings Southwest, 256 pp. $19.95

Opera! The Guide to Western Europe's Great Houses, 296 pp. $18.95

The People's Guide to Mexico, 10th ed., 608 pp. $19.95

Ranch Vacations: The Complete Guide to Guest and Resort, Fly-Fishing, and Cross-Country Skiing Ranches, 3rd ed., 512 pp. $19.95

The Shopper's Guide to Art and Crafts in the Hawaiian Islands, 272 pp. $13.95

Understanding Europeans, 272 pp. $14.95

Watch It Made in the U.S.A.: A Visitor's Guide to the Companies that Make Your Favorite Products, 328 pp. $16.95

Parenting Titles

Being a Father: Family, Work, and Self, 176 pp. $12.95

Teens: A Fresh Look, 240 pp. $14.95

Automotive Titles

The Greaseless Guide to Car Care, 2nd ed., 272 pp. $19.95

How to Keep Your Subaru Alive, 2nd ed., 480 pp. $21.95

How to Keep Your Toyota Pickup Alive, 392 pp. $21.95

How to Keep Your VW Alive, 25th Anniversary ed., 472 pp. $25

Ordering Information

Please check your local bookstore for our books, or call
1-800-888-7504
to order direct and to receive a complete catalog.
A shipping charge will be added to your order total.

Send all inquiries to:
John Muir Publications
P.O. Box 613
Santa Fe, NM 87504